EXPERIMENTS

IN PRIMARY EDUCATION

ASPECTS OF PROJECT FOLLOW-THROUGH

Experiments
in Primary Education
Aspects of Project Follow-Through

ELEANOR E. MACCOBY
Stanford University

MIRIAM ZELLNER
Social Science Research Council

Harcourt Brace Jovanovich, Inc.

NEW YORK · CHICAGO · SAN FRANCISCO · ATLANTA

This book grew out of a paper prepared for
the Committee on Learning and the Educational Process,
of the Social Science Research Council,
under a contract from the U.S. Department of Health, Education, and
Welfare, Office of Education (No. OEC-0-8-522495-4635).

ISBN: 0–15–526010-3

Library of Congress Catalog Card Number: 74–136969
Published 1970 by Harcourt Brace Jovanovich, Inc.
Printed in the United States of America

ACKNOWLEDGMENTS FOR ILLUSTRATIONS:
Cover photograph by Elaine Wickens;
ii and 94, courtesy of Arizona Center for Early Childhood Education, University of Arizona
2, courtesy of Education Development Center,
14, courtesy of New Century Educational Division of Meredith Corporation;
22, courtesy of Department of Human Development, University of Kansas;
32, courtesy of Bank Street College of Education, photograph by Elaine Wickens
58, courtesy of Yakima Public Schools, Yakima, Washington;
76, courtesy of Institute for Developmental Studies, New York University,
102, courtesy of Far West Laboratory for Educational Research and Development
114, courtesy of Learning Research and Development Center, University of Pittsburgh
126, courtesy of High/Scope Educational Research Foundation

PREFACE *

This book deals with experimental efforts to improve the quality of public school education for groups of children who have not benefited enough from the usual educational practices. Specifically, these pages focus on Project Follow-Through, a set of federally funded "intervention" programs for grade-school children who come from impoverished environments. Some of the programs are oriented toward bringing into general classroom use the technology that educators and psychologists already possess. Others emphasize the development of new technology. But changing and improving the educational process is much more than a technological matter. Persistent questions of values and objectives arise, involving the explosive issues of race and minority cultures. Moreover, in many communities educational innovation runs headlong into a struggle over who shall control the schools.

The purpose of this book is to compare the educational theories and values of a set of alternative approaches to compensatory education and to discuss the issues that arise when these theories and values are translated into everyday classroom practice in a setting of widespread social change. We try to analyze some of the psychological assumptions, educational philosophies, and pedagogical methods that underlie the programs and to convey especially the individual flavor of each program. We also discuss the numerous problems that arise as experimental programs are introduced into existing schools. We do not attempt to evaluate Project Follow-Through as a whole, to say whether it has produced gains in the academic achievement of the children involved, or to determine whether any one of the projects has been more effective than the others. It is too early for this. A nationwide evaluation of the programs is being carried out by the Stanford Research Institute at the time of this writing, and individual programs are also evaluating their own effectiveness. Only when the SRI study is completed will it be possible to begin to assess the nationwide success of Follow-Through. Only then will it be possible to make some judgments, albeit limited ones, about the relative success of the various experimental approaches in dealing with various kinds of children and in producing various kinds of gains. At present any judgments of this kind would be premature.

In the meantime, however, we believe that the experience of Follow-Through educators needs to be widely known. The lessons to be learned from the innovative efforts of the Follow-Through programs are especially applicable, of course, to those who are concerned with educating the children in the large urban "ghettos" and in other settings where minority-group children are clustered. But schools for these children are not the only ones in trouble during the present period of rapid social change; the issues faced in Follow-Through classrooms turn out to have implications for almost every classroom and almost every teacher. A chronicle of the activities and observations of those who have been on the firing line of "compensatory" education conveys a message about how complex a process it is to translate an educational theory into everyday classroom practice. Such a chronicle also conveys a message of hope: Though difficult, reform is possible.

This book grew out of a paper prepared for the Committee on Learning and the Educational Process, of the Social Science Research Council, under a contract from the U.S. Department of Health, Education, and Welfare, Office of Education. To obtain the information needed for a working paper on the nature of the psychological theories involved in existing programs of compensatory education, we interviewed program sponsors and studied the program documents describing their work. We also talked to some teachers and school administrators and visited some classrooms. In May 1969 the Subcommittee on Compensatory Education of the SSRC's Committee on Learning and the Educational Process conducted a conference attended by most of the Follow-Through teachers, as well as by some researchers, educators, sociologists, and child-development specialists not currently involved with Follow-Through. At this conference, the program sponsors commented on our summaries and interpretations of their programs, amplified their descriptions of their objectives and methods, and commented on one another's programs. In the course of these discussions, some of the differences among contrasting schools of thought became even sharper, while others turned out to be matters of emphasis only. Perhaps the most important theme emerging from these discussions was that the success of an educational intervention program depends on many things beyond the theory of teaching and learning that an educator has. All program directors encountered problems in implementing their objectives within the actual school system and felt that it was fully as important to understand the processes of institutional change as it was to understand the processes of successful instruction.

These discussions broadened our objectives for the present work. We felt it necessary to go beyond the analysis of the theoretical assumptions underlying the different approaches to pedagogy and to discuss some of the issues concerning school systems as institutions. We have done this with some diffidence. Systems analysis is not our area of expertise; moreover, a thorough treatment of the school systems' response to experimental intervention programs requires much more information than we collected in our interviews and observations. We hope that our descriptive report, based on the information that we did assemble, will generate some interest and a sense of the pressing need for "systems analysis" of school systems that are involved in innovative change.

This book reflects the contributions, at the conference and elsewhere, of many people. The program sponsors whose programs we summarize in Chapter 1 have been quoted at some length. We preferred to let the sponsors speak for themselves and their programs wherever possible. Their words reveal something of the differences of personality as well as viewpoint among programs; they also suggest the immediacy of the issues and problems the programs are facing and give a sense of the dialogue that must inevitably be part of any effort to evaluate and improve education. We hope that we have adequately represented what the sponsors wanted to say, and we are grateful for their willingness to find time in their extraordinarily busy schedules to be interviewed and to conduct us on classroom visits. Our gratitude, of course, extends to all the participants in the SSRC's Conference on Compensatory Education, held in May 1969; they are listed on page xii.

In addition, we have drawn on the views and work of the following teachers, school administrators, and researchers:

Charles Ascheim, Education Development Center, Newton, Massachusetts

Susan Bromberg, Bank Street College of Education, New York, New York

Joan Costello, Institute of Juvenile Research, Chicago, Illinois

Martin Deutsch, New York University, New York, New York

Richard Dunham, Florida State University, Tallahassee, Florida

Kenneth Haskins, St. Joseph's Elementary School, Boston, Massachusetts

Alice Paul, University of Arizona, Tucson, Arizona

Manuel Ramirez, Pitzer College, Claremont, California

Daniel Scheinfeld, University of Chicago, Chicago, Illinois

David Seeley, Public Education Association, New York, New York

Edna Shapiro, Bank Street College of Education, New York, New York

Halene Weaver, University of Arizona, Tucson, Arizona

The continuing support and guidance of the Follow-Through programs themselves comes, of course, from the U.S. Office of Education, under the direction of Dr. Robert Egbert. He and Dr. Richard Snyder, Chief of Research and Evaluation of Follow-Through, have given their sympathetic support and counsel to the preparation of this book, as have Dr. Henry Riecken and Dr. Rowland Mitchell, Jr., of the Social Science Research Council.

ELEANOR E. MACCOBY

MIRIAM ZELLNER

CONTENTS ✳

The following participated in the Conference on Compensatory Education, sponsored by the Committee on Learning and the Educational Process, of the Social Science Research Council, in May 1969. The affiliations shown are those held at the time of the conference:

DOROTHY ADKINS, University of Hawaii
RICHARD C. ANDERSON,* University of Illinois
WESLEY C. BECKER, University of Illinois
CARL E. BEREITER, The Ontario Institute for Studies in Education
GORDON H. BOWER,* Stanford University
DONALD G. BUSHELL, JR., University of Kansas
JOAN COSTELLO, Institute of Juvenile Research
LOIS-ELLIN DATTA, Office of Economic Opportunity, Head Start
RICHARD DE CHARMS, University of Washington
VICTOR H. DENENBERG, Purdue University
MARTIN DEUTSCH, New York University
RICHARD M. DUNHAM, Florida State University
ROBERT EGBERT, U.S. Office of Education
BARBARA D. FINBERG, Carnegie Corporation of New York
CATHERINE GARVEY, Johns Hopkins University
JACQUELINE GOODNOW, George Washington University
IRA J. GORDON, University of Florida
LASSAR G. GOTKIN, New Jersey State Education Department
IRVING GOTTESMAN, University of Minnesota
KENNETH HASKINS, Morgan School
RONALD HENDERSON, University of Arizona
ROBERT D. HESS, Stanford University
WAYNE H. HOLTZMAN,* University of Texas
MARIE M. HUGHES, University of Arizona
CHRISTOPHER JENCKS, Harvard University
JEROME KAGAN,* Harvard University
CONSTANCE K. KAMII, Ypsilanti Public Schools
ROBERT E. KLEIN, INCAP, Guatemala, C.A.
ELEANOR E. MACCOBY, Stanford University
MARJORIE MARTUS, Ford Foundation
JOHN W. MC DAVID, JR., University of Miami
SAMUEL MESSICK, Educational Testing Service
ROWLAND L. MITCHELL, JR., Social Science Research Council
LLOYD N. MORRISETT,* Carnegie Corporation of New York
FRANCIS H. PALMER, City University of New York
ALICE PAUL, University of Arizona
MANUEL RAMIREZ, Rice University
LAUREN B. RESNICK, University of Pittsburgh
HENRY W. RIECKEN, Social Science Research Council
EARL SCHAEFER, National Institute of Mental Health
DANIEL SCHEINFELD, University of Chicago
DAVID S. SEELEY, Public Education Association
IRVING SIGEL, Merrill-Palmer Institute
PHILIP H. SORENSEN, Stanford Research Institute
RICHARD SNYDER, U.S. Office of Education
HERBERT A. SPRIGLE, Psychological Clinic
SUSAN STODOLSKY, University of Chicago
FRED L. STRODTBECK, University of Chicago
HALENE WEAVER, University of Arizona
DAVID P. WEIKART, Ypsilanti Public Schools
JOHN N. M. WHITING, Harvard University
MIRIAM ZELLNER, Social Science Research Council
HERBERT ZIMILES, Bank Street College of Education

* Member of Committee on Learning and the Educational Process

EXPERIMENTS
IN PRIMARY EDUCATION
ASPECTS OF PROJECT FOLLOW-THROUGH

1 *

Introduction

This book deals with some of the experimental programs in Project Follow-Through, a nationwide effort to improve the grade-school education provided for children from impoverished environments. In it we describe how ten different Follow-Through programs have tried to bring about educational reform. We examine some of the psychological assumptions that underlie the programs and try to convey especially those characteristics of each program that differentiate it from the others. In later chapters we contrast the several educational philosophies and pedagogical methods and attempt to discover how the one leads to the other in day-to-day classroom settings. We also discuss how experimental programs are introduced into schools; what is involved in integrating a new program into an existing school system; and how experimental programs relate to the local community outside the school.

In this chapter we describe the Follow-Through programs that form the subject of this book. First, however, we turn to Project Follow-Through itself.

The Beginning of Project Follow-Through ✳

Project Follow-Through is closely related to Operation Head Start. Head Start began in 1965 as a massive, nationwide attempt to provide underprivileged children with preschool experiences that would enhance their ability to profit from public-school education. After several years of experience with Head Start, however, it became evident that although some short-term gains in children's intellectual performance could be produced during the preschool years, the children often lost whatever momentum had been generated by their Head Start experience once they had spent a year or two in a standard elementary school. We hasten to point out that the Head Start program is still young, and that it is by no means clear that its benefits will continue to be transitory. Indeed, some programs do seem to succeed in producing relatively long-lasting improvements in the learning ability of some of the children they serve. Nevertheless, there are many children who do "backslide." Does this occur because the whole concept of "compensatory education" in early childhood is unsound? Or is there something about elementary schools that fails to sustain and build upon genuine gains that the children have made in preschool?

Project Follow-Through is an attempt to answer the second question by modifying the programs offered to underprivileged children during their first four years of public school. Many but not all of the children in Follow-Through classrooms were previously enrolled in Head Start. Most are members of racial or cultural minorities. The Follow-Through program, funded on a much smaller scale than Head Start, is frankly experimental. It is based on the assumption that we do not know very much about why our public schools have failed to produce an acceptable level of academic achievement in millions of youngsters growing up in the big cities and rural backwaters of our nation. The Follow-Through program has been open to innovation. People with a wide range of ideas about how classroom procedures (or, for that matter, whole school systems) might be modified so as to teach these children more effectively have been encouraged to apply for modest Follow-Through funds to try out their programs. Pilot programs went into operation during the academic year 1967–68.

Beginning in the fall of 1968, many of the experimental classrooms came under the direction of "program sponsors." A program sponsor is a professional person, an educator or psychologist, who may or may not be associated with a university. On the basis of a specific educational philosophy, he works out a curriculum and a set of teacher-training procedures and takes responsibility for seeing that his procedures go into effect in a given set of classrooms. He also takes responsibility for the continued training and supervision of the teachers and for monitoring the children's progress throughout the life of the program. Some sponsors direct classrooms in widely scattered locations. One sponsor, for example, has put his program into effect in schools on several Indian reservations in the South and Southwest and, in addition, supervises classrooms in Los Angeles, Baltimore, Newark, and in several smaller towns and cities in North Carolina, Georgia, Iowa, Indiana, Texas, New Mexico, and Alaska. Several large cities have more than one sponsor operating classrooms in different parts of their large school establishment. Some sponsors are interested in trying out their educational procedures with a variety of ethnic groups, in order to compare the effectiveness of different procedures in different settings; others prefer to concentrate their work with a single population group. A few Follow-Through programs are "self-sponsored." This simply means that a community group applies for financial support to try out a new approach to compensatory education, without inviting an outside sponsor to direct it. Self-sponsored programs are sometimes confined to a single school.

In this book we discuss ten of the sponsored Follow-Through programs. To acquaint the reader with them and to illustrate the diversity of educational philosophies in Follow-Through, brief descriptions of the programs appear below.

THE PROGRAMS *

Although the description that follows cannot possibly do full justice to the subtleties within and among these Follow-Through programs, it will serve as an introduction to the basic approach each program takes.

While some programs clearly bear the stamp of the personality and viewpoints of the director, others have more the quality of group products and should not be identified with one or two individuals. Nevertheless, for the sake of convenience, we shall generally follow the practice, common among workers in the field, of referring to the programs by their sponsors' names.

The EDC Approach

DAVID ARMINGTON, SPONSOR
Education Development Center, Newton, Massachusetts

Perhaps the essential feature of Armington's EDC approach is an emphasis on self-development, and this holds for teachers and schools as well as for children. Much of the program's inspiration is drawn from the revolution in British Infant Schools. Each class is encouraged to develop its own personality by being responsive to the needs and interests of the children and the talents and style of the teacher.

A fundamental educational aim is for children to assume responsibility for their own learning. There is a rich environment of materials for children to explore. They are encouraged to initiate activities, be self-directing, and become intensely involved in their interests. Typically, there is a variety of activities going on, much of them interdisciplinary. The time schedule is flexible, permitting children to learn according to their individual rhythms of engagement and disengagement. The theme of self-management also finds expression in a social environment of cooperation where children work together and learn from one another.

The teacher is seen as a responsive, insightful human being who likes children and enters into their growth, not as someone who directs or is a sideline spectator, but as a guide who is constantly involved. Her objective is to get the children involved in things that are relevant to them. The EDC program prescribes no one way to do this. It is an environment in which all things are potentially legitimate, even, at times, workbooks and programed learning, although reliance on a structured, "prepackaged" curriculum is strongly resisted.

The content of what is taught is strongly influenced by local conditions and objectives. It is believed that skills like reading and writing develop more surely if they are not treated as academic exercises but are taught in rich environments that stimulate the children's imagination and thought and foster their desire to communicate. All forms of expressive representation, in the arts and in movement as well as in language, are considered valid and important.

An important component of the EDC approach is an advisory team, whose task is to help school systems put this philosophy of education into practice and to help teachers learn to regard themselves as researchers and experimenters in the classroom. The team works by responding to the demands of a situation: It does not tell people what to do; it tries to help them do what they want and to extend what they are capable of doing.

The E-B or Engelmann-Becker Program

WESLEY BECKER, SPONSOR
Department of Educational Psychology, University of Illinois, Urbana, Illinois
A N D
SIEGFRIED ENGELMANN, SPONSOR
Institute for Research on Exceptional Children, Champaign, Illinois

The E-B program starts with the premise that disadvantaged children are academically behind middle-class children; in order to catch up, they must learn at a faster rate than middle-class children are learning. This reasoning leads Engelmann and Becker to the position that the primary concern of a compensatory program is to teach academic skills, and teach them rapidly.

At least one hour a day is spent on academic skills—twenty to thirty minutes each on reading, arithmetic, and language. Many procedures are used to train and ensure the attention of the children. The use of reinforcement is a key element of the program. Children are smiled at or praised for correct performance, and there is a conscious effort to make these "social reinforcers" contingent on the child's accomplishing the academic tasks set out for him. The teacher sits with four to six children and leads them in a quickly paced lesson of questions and responses. The materials are programed so that the children will not encounter tasks that are too difficult. The teacher receives continuous feedback on the performance of the children. Later skills in the curriculum depend on mastery of earlier skills, so the teacher makes sure that each skill is thoroughly mastered before she moves on to the next.

The E-B curriculum is carefully planned to facilitate the acquisition of generalized response systems that will apply to a whole set of problems. For example, the children learn the sounds that letters stand for and this enables them to read words they have never seen. The concept of an "average" is taught using a fulcrum and a set of weights that balance around the fulcrum. By stressing the relationship between a fulcrum and an equal sign, the children can generalize among multiplication, average, and lever problems. Paying attention to a task is also regarded as a generalized response set that can be reinforced and learned.

Engelmann and Becker believe that children will learn if they are taught well and there is a payoff for learning. No distinction is made between intrinsic and extrinsic motivation. While they recognize that it is important for children to want to learn, the assumption is that this motivation can be taught and one should not rely on its automatic presence or wait for it to develop spontaneously.

The E-B program places particular emphasis on remedying language deficiencies. The children in the program have difficulty, for instance, in using articles, conjunctions, prepositions, and small verbs; they do not seem to know the meaning of "not" or of relational terms such as "between" and "under." The language-training program, rather than concentrating on the social and expressive uses of language, teaches the concepts used in logical thinking, reading, and arithmetic. The other uses, it is believed, will develop incidentally. Likewise, Engelmann and Becker reason that it is not necessary to make a special effort to raise the self-esteem of the children; they believe that high self-esteem will be a by-product of competence.

The Behavior Analysis Program

DONALD BUSHELL, JR., SPONSOR
Department of Human Development, University of Kansas,
Lawrence, Kansas

Bushell's Behavior Analysis Program uses systematic reinforcement procedures to teach children the skills they need to compete effectively in school. These include skill in taking the social role of the student (knowing when to talk and when to be silent, staying with assigned tasks, and responding appropriately to praise), as well as the academic skills of language, reading, writing, and mathematics.

Bushell holds that an effective system of reinforcement makes the reward contingent on improved academic or social behavior. Typical rewards in his program include recess, snacks, art, and stories. For maximum effect, reinforcement must be delivered immediately, but since the immediate delivery of a story, for example, might terminate rather than strengthen the behavior on which it is contingent, a token economy has been instituted in some classrooms. Tokens (along with praise) can be dispensed immediately, contingent on appropriate behavior, and they can then be exchanged for preferred activities when these are available.

Bushell does not see the token system as precluding the possibility that learning in itself can be rewarding for a child. The tokens are only used to support the child's early efforts until he reaches a level of mastery that will allow him to enjoy, and be reinforced by, his new skill.

The teacher's role is that of a behavior modifier. If a child has earned too few tokens, the teacher knows something is wrong. She has not been paying sufficient attention to the child, she has assigned a task that is too difficult, or the available activities are not adequate reinforcers for that child. Thus, the token system checks the teacher's behavior as well as motivates the child's.

In this program parents are hired to function as behavior modifiers. Two parents participate in each classroom for five to seven weeks and then train two other parents to replace them. In addition to introducing positive reinforcement procedures to the parents, this practice substantially reduces the teacher-pupil ratio and correspondingly increases the reinforcement density possible.

In Bushell's program the progress of each child is monitored as closely as possible, and each child is encouraged to progress at his own maximum rate. To identify progress it is necessary to know both where the child started and where he is going. By emphasizing programed instructional materials that allow for individualized instruction, the teacher can easily monitor individual rates of progress.

The Bank Street Program

ELIZABETH GILKESON, SPONSOR
Bank Street College of Education, New York, New York
AND
HERBERT ZIMILES, SPONSOR
Bank Street College of Education, New York, New York

The Bank Street approach is concerned with many dimensions of each child's development. Learning and development are seen as intertwined, for if learning is to be more than superficial, it must be pursued by the child on behalf of his own development. The teacher is regarded as highly important in the learning-development process, since it is she who helps the child become aware of his world. She sensitizes him to his experiences, to sights, sounds, feelings, and ideas. She functions for the child as a consistent adult whom he learns to trust. At Bank Street it is believed that the learning of specific skills should not take place independently of healthy emotional development. A program that concentrates only on cognitive development would be doomed, since children, especially disadvantaged children with their frequently chaotic histories, need first of all to be able to trust in the predictability of the school environment and to learn the effects of their own actions within it. Only then are they able to persist at and profit from their work. The child must also be able to relate his in-school learning to his out-of-school learning, which requires mutual planning with parents.

Bank Street treats the classroom as the child's workroom, where he is free to investigate objects and explore various media. He makes choices and carries out plans. He works individually or undertakes cooperative projects. It is a stable, ordered environment. The teacher introduces activities and plans events, but her teaching is in terms of the individual child's response. She teaches diagnostically and plans individualized follow-up. She points out and elaborates on a child's experiences. The planned activities originate from classroom themes (organizing chores, cooking, block building) and later extend to community themes (food marketing, traffic control, sources of water). Academic skills are learned in the context of a relevant, engaging classroom life.

In this program language development is seen as including the development of interpersonal communication in addition to its role in cognitive development. Verbal communication is part of and a continuation of the child's experiences in communicating with people. Language as related to cognitive development also has its precursors, and these include the knowledge that the child has already acquired of the world and experiences he has had with things that stand for other things. Language, written and spoken, surrounds the child in the classroom, and the program's objective is that he will learn it as a useful, pleasurable tool.

The Florida Project

IRA GORDON, SPONSOR
Institute for Development of Human Resources,
College of Education, University of Florida, Gainesville, Florida

Gordon's position is that if an intervention program is to be successful, it must start early (preferably during infancy), and it must include the home environment, especially the mother, in addition to the child.

The language of disadvantaged children often shows a lack of comprehension of abstract and causal relationships. The children are impulsive and distractable; they have low self-esteem. Gordon feels that these deficits are related to the fact that the children's mothers do not provide models of abstract thinking for them; the mothers have difficulty organizing their own existences and create disordered homes for their children; and they, too, have low self-esteem and feel they have little control over their own fate. It is not enough to change the way the school teaches the children; one must also change the way their mothers teach them.

In Gordon's program teaching occurs in both the home and the school and is coordinated by a paid parent educator, who comes from the same population as the children's mothers. The parent educator is trained by the program personnel. In the classroom she functions as a teacher's aide. She then takes into the home the tasks that are taught in the classroom and instructs the mother in how to teach them to the child. The mother thus learns that education occurs in the home. She learns what kinds of child activities she should encourage, and she learns, as she observes her child learn, that her actions can have an effect and that she can be successful.

The curriculum is not standardized throughout the program, but it does have an orientation toward the theories of Jean Piaget. The children learn to arrange items in series, to classify, and to name. Tasks related to Piagetian stages are progressively sequenced and are demonstrated in a variety of contexts. For example, a systematic attempt is made to enumerate all the ways the toys and objects in the classroom can be used. Then the child is helped to discover and explore the alternatives himself, thus learning to be experimental rather than repetitious. The teacher or aide constantly uses language to accompany the child's actions. The child needs to hear the words that describe what he is doing if he is to become expressive himself. The parent educator and teacher are also encouraged to participate in curriculum design, especially in devising methods for dealing with the difficulties of individual children. Gordon's program makes no deliberate attempt to shape the child's behavior through the use of incentives. Mastery, it is felt, is its own reward.

The Instructional Games Program

LASSAR GOTKIN, SPONSOR
School of Education, Institute for Developmental Studies,
New York University, New York, New York

The most distinctive feature of Gotkin's games approach involves the development and use of games, game formats, and gamelike orientations as the central teaching method. An example is the Matrix Games curriculum, which teaches concepts and classifications skills and language. A typical picture matrix consists of four rows and four columns with some characteristic unique to each row and each column. In the example shown on the next page, the children might be directed (or direct one another) to "put a blue circle on two boys drinking milk." The cognitive requirements increase in complexity as the children gain facility with the task. For example, sequencing may be introduced by instructing the child: *"First* put a blue circle on two boys drinking milk, *then* put a red X on one girl putting on her hat." Or the teacher might cover up one of the squares and ask the children to figure out what her "secret" picture is.

    In developing games, Gotkin takes advantage of the principles of programed instruction: clear specification of instructional objectives, careful sequencing from simple to complex, small steps that virtually ensure errorless learning, active participation by the learner, and feedback on the correctness of a response.

A matrix from the Matrix Games.

In addition to providing a logical learning sequence, the games also establish what is thought to be a desirable social context. Children are taught to assume leadership roles and to organize their own learning. A group of children can easily manage themselves because each game has clearly defined rules and each child knows what is expected of him. The teacher, meanwhile, is freed to devote individualized attention to other children or to instruct another small group. Moreover, the nature of game structures permits semiprofessionals to teach and interact with children in significant ways; the program's intent is that this shall lead toward developing classroom environments in which the teacher is the leader of an instructional team.

In Gotkin's view, one reason why children from black ghetto neighborhoods fail in school is that the schools oppose what he calls the "rhythm" of the black culture. Black people have a style that is reflected in much of their behavior; many schools have rejected this. Gotkin is now incorporating into his curriculum the rhythmic noncompetitive games that are part of the black heritage and the culture of the streets.

In general, Gotkin is more impressed by the wide range in learning and learning abilities among "disadvantaged" children than by the fact that on the average they are behind their middle-class counterparts. He points out that games are flexible enough for several children of varied abilities to play together, each proceeding at his own pace.

The Tucson Early Education Model

MARIE HUGHES, SPONSOR
Arizona Center for Early Childhood Education,
College of Education, University of Arizona, Tucson, Arizona

AND

RONALD HENDERSON, SPONSOR
Arizona Center for Early Childhood Education,
College of Education, University of Arizona, Tucson, Arizona

According to Marie Hughes and Ronald Henderson, the Mexican-American children for whom their program was originally developed are deficient in both Spanish and English, have little experience in manipulating objects, and have little sense of time as an ordered sequence of events (many have difficulty narrating a sequential tale, or planning a sequence of actions). The objectives of the program include remedying these deficiencies.

The Tucson curriculum is kept flexible. Teaching elaborates on and explores what is already salient for the children—their environment and their current interests. There is relatively less emphasis on which items are taught and on the transmission of specific content, and more emphasis on "learning to learn."

The teacher is to be at the service of the child to help him in his learning. She does not insist that he perform as she wishes, and rather than criticize him when he is wrong, she capitalizes on what he has done well and helps him to perform correctly. When she praises him, she lets him know that he is progressing. The child is encouraged to use all available sources for learning: The classroom environment is there to be explored. One program objective is that the children learn to cooperate with each other in their work.

Hughes and Henderson emphasize language training, but it is not taught word by word in formal lessons. The program's philosophy is that if language is made useful, and if language and the written word surround the child, he will easily learn. The children's stories are recorded and the class's experiences are set down in illustrated books. When they start to write on their own, their work is displayed with the mistakes left unaltered. Direct correction is felt to discourage communication; providing language models (the teacher, books) for the child to imitate will serve to correct mistakes as the child progresses.

The Tucson philosophy is that the child does not have to be forced, or even requested, to learn. It is believed that if the environment is sufficiently interesting it will of itself, and without any prodding from the teacher, "demand" that the child learn.

The program encompasses four main objectives: (1) language competence, including labeling and concept development; (2) an intellectual base of other skills necessary for learning, including the ability to attend, to recall, to organize, to choose, and to imitate; (3) a motivational base, including positive attitudes toward school and learning, the ability to persist, and the expectation of success; and (4) societal arts and skills, which include language and mathematics as well as social cooperation. Ideally, these goals are developed simultaneously in activities that are meaningful for the child. For example, a teacher who is making ice cream with a small group of children is teaching how to sequence, new words, new concepts, and new technical and social skills. She is also developing the children's attitudes toward learning.

The Responsive Model

GLEN NIMNICHT, SPONSOR
Far West Laboratory for Educational Research and Development,
Berkeley, California

In his program, Nimnicht would like to help develop individuals who have both the ability to solve problems on their own and the confidence to attack them. To this end, his program concentrates on enhancing the child's intellect, his sense of autonomy, and his self-concept.

The classroom environment is structured so that as the child freely explores it, he will make discoveries from which he will learn. For example, by experimenting with the programed typewriter (originally devised by O. K. Moore), the child learns to read and write; at the same time he is learning to find answers to problems by himself. Nimnicht favors "autotelic" activities: that is, activities that are self-rewarding and do not depend upon rewards or punishments that are unrelated to the activities themselves. Nimnicht also feels "responsiveness" is important: The environment in which these activities take place should be responsive to the child—it should respond when he is interested in learning and give him immediate feedback from his problem-solving attempts. Similarly, the teacher is trained to be responsive to the child. She guides him in response to his expressions of interest and helps him find answers, but avoids giving them to him. When she thinks it is appropriate to teach a particular concept or bit of knowledge, she does so by making use of and elaborating on what the child is interested in.

In addition to problem solving and concept formation, Nimnicht's curriculum stresses sensory and perceptual acuity, which is considered an important part of cognitive development. The assumption is that disadvantaged children often come from crowded and noisy homes where their sensory experience is largely undifferentiated. In contrast, the classroom fosters sensory and perceptual discrimination through its orderliness and the tasks it contains. The child can focus on activities and can see and hear without distractions. The teacher further differentiates the environment for the child by providing verbal mediation to help him understand in words what he is perceiving.

Another assumption in Nimnicht's program is that disadvantaged children, as compared with middle-class children, have suffered in the quantity and quality of their interaction with adults. There is less contact, and that which does occur is of poorer quality because the parents themselves are uneducated and often psychologically defeated. Nimnicht is consequently very concerned that his program instill in the children not only the learning skills they will need but also the positive self-concept that will allow them to expect and work toward mastery. He avoids using methods that will undermine this goal. Extrinsic reinforcers are not used because it is believed that they inevitably imply differential reward—a gold star for one child is equivalent to differential punishment or a failure experience for another child. Nimnicht's autotelic system is based, rather, on the principle of intrinsic motivation. A child learns because he wants to.

The Primary Education Project

LAUREN RESNICK, SPONSOR
Learning Research and Development Center,
University of Pittsburgh, Pittsburgh, Pennsylvania

Resnick's program is based on the proposition that if a child is to learn most efficiently, he must be allowed to proceed through the curriculum at his own rate. If the curriculum is to teach most efficiently, its components must be carefully, optimally sequenced.

The curriculum is constructed by using a process called component analysis. First, some stated educational objective is set, such as what the child should be able to do when he finishes second grade. The skills are clearly specified in behavioral terms. Each skill identified is then analyzed to determine what lower-level skills are prerequisite to it. Each of the lower-level skills is in turn analyzed to determine its prerequisites, and so on, thus generating a hierarchy of objectives. The hierarchy is derived both from the use of logic and from a knowledge of psychology, such as Piaget's observations provide.

Tests are constructed to determine whether or not the child possesses each of the skills identified. This testing procedure serves several functions: It diagnoses very precisely where the child stands, what his progress has been, and what the next pedagogical step must be. It also measures the teacher's success, and it tests the adequacy of the component analysis procedure (any child who has a given skill should also have all its prerequisite skills).

Resnick considers three general classes of skills to be particularly important for inclusion in the curriculum. These skills are thought to underlie all higher-order conceptual functioning. The first is orienting and attending skills. These are necessary if the child is to learn and to function in the classroom: He must be able to attend to a task, follow directions, and the like. The second class of skills is the perceptual-motor, including gross and fine motor skills, as well as the visual and auditory skills that are so closely tied to the child's earliest concepts (colors, shapes, sounds). Thirdly, there are conceptual-linguistic skills, including classification, reasoning, memory, language, and early mathematical concepts.

By and large, Resnick feels that the child learns by interacting with materials and with other children, rather than learning directly from the teacher. The teacher's function is to reinforce the child's efforts and successes and to make sure he gets assistance when he needs it. The diagnostic tests, which monitor learning, enable the teacher to be eclectic in the specifics of the curriculum and still not lose sight of her goals. The tasks given to the child are designed to teach him the next skills he needs, according to the component analysis. To keep the child working, the least powerful reinforcer that is effective is used—praise, gold stars, or tokens. As time goes on, the child is able to work more and more independently of reinforcement.

The Cognitively Oriented Approach

DAVID WEIKART, SPONSOR

Ypsilanti Public Schools, Ypsilanti, Michigan

Weikart's program focuses on three major concerns: the curriculum, which is cognitively oriented; the teacher, who is encouraged to take an active and innovative role in developing a program for her class; and the home, where teachers encourage the mothers to promote the cognitive growth of their children.

The curriculum is derived from the theories of Piaget: Conceptual development is understood to move from the simple to the complex and from the concrete to the abstract. The child progresses from the motor level of abstraction, where he learns to use his own body to experience concepts, to the verbal level, where he learns to label what he is doing or experiencing, and finally to the symbolic level, where through familiarity with objects and object representations he develops the skills necessary to think abstractly. Self-concept is one of the most important concepts the child learns. The teacher can assist him in this learning by treating him as an autonomous individual who can make choices for himself. The teacher also demonstrates language uses for the child by labeling, using prepositions, interpreting actions, and explaining causal relations.

Weikart believes that teachers can be effective only when the supervising staff has respect for them. He recognizes that without the teachers' cooperative participation even the very best curriculum is doomed. Within the Weikart program the teacher has the acknowledged right to design her own program for her own class, developing goals and methods through interaction with other teachers and through critical evaluation and guidance from the supervising staff.

In addition to the classroom curriculum, home training is seen as a necessary part of the program. The mother usually has command of the language and the concepts necessary to teach her child, but she needs to be encouraged to *use* her intellectual skills in talking to the child and in becoming involved in his cognitive growth. The teacher suggests tasks for the mother to present to the child and ways in which the mother can more effectively teach him.

As the above sketches of the various programs indicate, there are many points of similarity among the programs, as well as some rather profound points of difference. Each program has its own central emphasis. In Chapter 2 we examine these more closely.

2 *

Similarities and Differences among Follow-Through Programs

In this chapter we sketch the major theoretical viewpoints to be found in Follow-Through. We point out the issues on which there is substantial agreement and begin to explore those on which there is substantial disagreement.

Points of Agreement among Programs *

Certain basic assumptions concerning teaching and learning pervade all the programs, regardless of their theoretical orientations. Some of these are as follows:

(1) Education must begin from the child's level at the time of his entry into the program. It is necessary to assess the child's capabilities in detail at this time and to adapt the program to what the assessment shows.

(2) Since children—even children from the "same" environment—differ greatly in both their repertoire of previously learned

skills and in the content of what has been learned, teaching should be individualized to the greatest possible extent.

(3) "Culturally deprived" children can and do learn the essential material presented in any reasonable school curriculum under the right conditions. If an individual child is not learning, the fault lies in the materials being presented to him or in the way they are being presented, not in the child.

Point 3 needs some amplification. No one doubts that a few of the children growing up in impoverished environments are mentally retarded. By this we mean that some of the children suffer from birth defects or other biological abnormalities that impair their intellectual functioning. Every social group produces some such children. The culture of poverty probably produces more than its share, considering that among impoverished women there is a high rate of disease and malnutrition during pregnancy and a high rate of difficult deliveries. However, the large majority of children born into a depriving environment are not damaged in this sense. It is a cornerstone assumption of the compensatory education movement as a whole that the children from such environments are educable, but that the circumstances of their lives are such that they often do not acquire some of the skills and motivations that underlie success in school. There is considerable debate concerning the nature of their deficit, and more will be said about this below. But the assumption is that if educators can identify correctly what it is the children need to know, good teaching will remedy the deficiencies to a significant degree. No one claims that compensatory education programs can wipe out the culture of poverty in one generation. But people who have been involved with experimental intervention programs generally share the feeling that although there are some approaches that do not work, there are some that do, and that we are beginning to learn how to get acceptable levels of school performance from "deprived" children. Many feel that the learning capacity of poor children has been grossly underrated.

(4) Any program, to be successful, must specify its objectives in detail, describing the skills and knowledge it wants the children to have when certain teaching procedures have been carried

out. There is a good deal of agreement among programs in what these objectives are.

(5) For a child to be successfully taught, he must have certain "school-appropriate" behaviors, such as being able to pay attention to the tasks for reasonable periods of time. Also, he must avoid behavior that will disrupt his own learning and that of other children, such as running around at inappropriate times, making too much noise, or fighting. Above all, he must be motivated to learn. A program must be concerned with these larger task-orientation matters as well as with specific content.

(6) Children should enjoy school and experience success within it. Ideally, punishment should be eliminated, and a child should never be made to feel that he is a failure. He cannot learn successfully if he is afraid of the teacher, the school, or of learning itself.

Differences among Programs ✻

As is obvious from Chapter 1, the educational philosophies embodied in Follow-Through programs are enormously varied. Any attempt to classify them does violence to subtle differences that may be crucially important. Nevertheless, one can identify certain major groups of programs and schools of thought:

(1) Programs oriented toward behavior modification. Performance on intellectual tasks is thought of as a class of behavior subject to the same laws that govern other kinds of behavior. *Education is, or should be, a process of reinforcing children for the desired behavior.*

(2) Programs oriented toward cognitive growth. Performance on intellectual tasks is thought of as reflecting the level of development of mental structures and operations. *Education is, or should be, a process of facilitating the normal stage-wise growth of these processes.*

(3) Programs oriented toward self-actualization. Performance on intellectual tasks reflects whether a child has chosen to master the tested-for contents in pursuit of his own goals. *Educa-*

tion is, or should be, a process of stimulating the child's intellectual curiosity, providing him with a range of experiences and materials appropriate to his existing skills, so that he can learn to become competent in his own physical and social environment.

(4) There is a fourth kind of program, which emphasizes changing the locus of control over the schools. None of the ten programs described in Chapter 1 has this as a central theme, although they all recognize the importance of the socio-political context in which an educational experiment occurs. There are other Follow-Through programs in which the issues of power and changes in power are paramount. A basic assumption of these programs is that performance on intellectual tasks reflects whether a child has a sense of self-worth, and that this is largely determined by whether the people in charge of educating him respect him and really want to educate him. From this point of view, past failures of schools with "disadvantaged" children do not reflect deficits in the children. Rather, they result from maladaptive school bureaucracies and ambivalent attitudes among school personnel toward the minority-group children in their charge. *The educational system must be responsive to the needs and wishes of the community being served. If this condition is met, any of the three educational approaches listed above will work.*

Aside from these differences in underlying educational philosophies, programs differ in their specific objectives. Some programs take it as their primary task to transmit a body of knowledge and skills. Others are less interested in the specifics of what is learned and feel that their mission is to teach a child *how* to learn—to transform him into a person who will be a relatively autonomous learner, who will know how to go about solving whatever problem he is working on and where to go for the information he needs. If he develops these abilities, it is argued, he can be counted on to acquire specific knowledge whenever he needs it. The "content" versus "learning to learn" objectives are not mutually exclusive, of course.

The stress on autonomy in a few programs, not described here, extends to the view that an educational program ought to make children independent enough to resist being led into behavior that is "absurd" (as Paul Goodman uses the word). A truly autonomous child may be more difficult for a school system to handle. He may refuse to learn some of the traditional subject matter presented to him, or refuse to be tested on materials he deems irrelevant; he may not display the conforming, competitive kind of achievement motivation characteristic of the "best" products of most current school systems.

A somewhat more muted approach to autonomy is found in Follow-Through programs that stress that there are proper times to "go along" with what is required, even though it may not seem entirely relevant to the learner at the moment, and times to resist. Such programs emphasize that education should help children learn to make intelligent, discriminative, decisions about which is the desirable stance to take in specific instances. Hughes, of the Tucson program, expresses this philosophy:

> We want children to say "No" when someone suggests that the windows of a vacant house be broken, or to be able to resist joining their adolescent friends in a visit to a tavern of questionable reputation. We want them to be able to spend some time alone in a profitable manner, as well as to be members of some friendship group. The studies of our most constructive and creative people have shown them [to be] autonomous but also discriminative. It is this distinction that is of major importance in the socialization of children. There are consequences that follow whatever one does. The assessment of such consequences is a necessary process for children to learn.

Some differences among programs arise out of differing views about why the disadvantaged child achieves poorly in school. There is fairly general agreement on the fact that, although there may be a great deal wrong with the way the schools have gone about trying to educate these children, the children already show a deficit at the time they enter school. What precisely is implied in the notion of "deficit"? In a certain sense, all children—from advantaged as well as disadvantaged homes—come to school with deficits. For example, most of them cannot read, and from the standpoint of the demands of the adult culture, this is a deficit—

one that the school is designed to correct. Obviously, the term as applied to children in Head Start and Follow-Through programs means something more than simply that there are many things they do not know. The term implies, first, that their level of knowledge and skill is below that of the "average" child of school-entry age— below the level that the usual first-grade curriculum demands. Another way of putting it is to say that existing first-grade curricula are not usually designed to remedy the particular deficits that many of these children have. Secondly, the term "deficit" sometimes implies that the ability to acquire the necessary knowledge and skills has somehow been impaired and must be corrected by special orientation and training of the child in the very process of learning itself.

A great deal has been said about the precise nature of the deficits that characterize poor school achievers from impoverished homes. Carl Bereiter and Engelmann† have discussed the matter in detail, focusing on language deficit as the major problem. There is fairly general agreement that the problem of poor school achievers has something to do with the lack of development of certain language skills. It is interesting that in the case of children for whom English is a second language, or children who speak a strong dialect, the problem does not stem entirely from the school's failure to use their first language (although this contributes strongly to the school difficulties of children in certain communities). It is sometimes found that children are deficient in the use of their own first language or dialect. It appears to be true, then, that there is something about the culture of poverty that fails to stimulate the growth of certain kinds of verbal concepts, or, most importantly, fails to stimulate the *use* of these concepts for planning and guiding action, at least among some children.

How and why do these deficiencies come about? When one poses this question, one encounters an important disagreement among educators. Some feel it is not a question that needs answering. Their reasoning goes this way: "Let us take the children

† Carl Bereiter and Siegfried Engelmann, *Teaching Disadvantaged Children in the Preschool* (Englewood Cliffs, N.J.: Prentice-Hall, 1966).

where they are. Let us find out what they can and cannot do, and start teaching them what they need to know. If a given child speaks very little, cannot use negatives, and does not understand the meaning of 'under' or 'around,' it doesn't matter whether this is true because his father left the home when he was an infant, or because his mother works or has so many children that she doesn't have time to talk to him. It doesn't even matter whether the child has been rejected and unloved. We are not going to be able to change his history anyhow, so let's not spend time trying to find out exactly what made him the way he is. Let us use our energies trying to give him the tools he needs to be an effective person from now on."

The alternative position is that we do indeed need to know about causes. The reasoning behind this position is as follows: "Some children growing up in impoverished homes are effective learners when they come to school. Others are not. There is reason to believe that the difference lies somewhere in the nature of the interactions among the members of the family—particularly in the nature of the mother's interaction with the child. If we can find ways to reach into the home and change this pattern, we will have made more efficient use of our resources. For one thing, there will be a better chance that any gains made in the classroom will be enduring and self-sustaining, once we have remedied the home conditions that were hampering the child's progress and pulling him back. Furthermore, we help the younger children of this family, not just the one who currently happens to be in Head Start or Follow-Through." Proponents of this view include parent education as an integral part of their efforts to educate the children. More will be said below about the ways in which this has been done. Here it is sufficient to note that there are important differences in point of view concerning how far back in the causal chain one needs to go in seeking a remedy for educational deficiencies. Some feel that it is necessary to go all the way back to the conditions that produce the defective interaction patterns one finds in many impoverished families. The implications of these differences in strategy will be encountered frequently in the following chapters.

Differences in Psychological Theory ✳

Some differences among programs stem not so much from different objectives or strategies as from different psychological theories about the nature of learning and motivation.

Two theories that have had considerable influence on the compensatory education programs are (1) reinforcement learning theory (in the tradition of B. F. Skinner) and (2) cognitive development theory (derived in part from Jean Piaget). We should point out that a number of leading proponents of reinforcement theory (such as Engelmann) were not directly influenced by Skinner, at least not initially, while others were. Although we recognize that some practitioners of this approach have developed teaching strategies that could not have been derived directly from preexisting Skinnerian research and theory, their strategies may be seen to be consistent with the theory once they are invented. There is a coherent body of theory here that does guide educational practice. For the sake of brevity and simplicity, we will use the terms "Skinnerian" and "behavior modifier" interchangeably to designate followers of reinforcement learning theory.

"Cognitive-developmental" theories may be subdivided into two main classes: those that concern themselves primarily with intellectual growth, and those that stress the interrelationships between intellectual processes and social-emotional growth. The Bank Street approach, for example, falls into the second class. It has much in common with Piagetian programs, but also draws upon a long tradition growing out of Dewey's educational philosophy and the principles of dynamic developmental theory. Their approach developed out of the progressive educational movement of the thirties. The Bank Street viewpoint has been the dominant theme in American nursery-school education for many years, and in Follow-Through it is being adapted to primary-school, non-middle-class children.

Another school of thought that falls into the second class stresses the importance of autonomous motivation as well as the interrelatedness of feeling and thought. This philosophy has its strongest exemplars in the British Infant Schools. The Follow-Through program that stems most directly from this tradition is Armington's EDC program.

It is fruitless, however, to discuss how closely any given program conforms to the gospel as set forth by Skinner, Piaget, or Dewey. More important for our purposes is this question: How have the exponents of these theories understood them and brought them to bear in the classroom? This is the question we take up in Chapter 3.

3*

Views about Learning: What It Is, How It Occurs, and What Should Be Learned

When one watches a teacher at work with children, can one tell what particular philosophy of education inspired her training and produced the materials she uses? We delineate some of the major theoretical differences in educational philosophy and then describe the differences and similarities in procedures that appear to result.

Behavior Modification or Cognitive Development? *

The cognitive-developmentalist, following Piagetian theory, believes that the process of education is one of building cognitive structures in the mind of the child. The behavior modifier, following the theories of B. F. Skinner, is wont to say that he does not know what cognitive structures are—that he believes these are fictions, myths, invented by the psychologist that serve more to hinder than to help his understanding of how the child learns. The Skinnerian conceives of education as a process of producing changes in observable behavior. Usually the changes take the form of adding new responses to the child's repertoire—like filling up an empty jar with marbles, adding one marble at a time. The Skinnerian thinks of behavior as being under stimulus control and holds that education consists in bringing specified behavior under the control of specified stimuli. Reinforcement is the mechanism that produces this result. The Skinnerian does not, of course, believe that the child has no brain or that nothing goes on inside the head—only that it is not profitable to speculate about these internal processes, since they cannot be directly observed or controlled. The only thing we can control is what we observe, and all we can observe is behavior.

The Piagetian does not conceive of the child as being under stimulus control. On the contrary, to put the issue in its most extreme form, he conceives of stimuli as being under the control of the child. More stimuli are always present in the stimulus complex that surrounds the child than he can respond to. The child selects portions of the available array according to what he needs for his ongoing activity. He not only selects, but interprets what is selected in terms of his previously stored experience. This experience is stored in the form of internal "structures" or "schemata" that guide the processes of perceiving and conceiving. These "structures," in turn, are reorganized on the basis of new experiences that cannot be dealt with through existing structures. The selected data from the environment are classified and operated upon with varying degrees of sophistication, depending upon the child's level of cognitive development, that is, upon his existing schemata. If a child does not have (wholly or in large part) the internal structures or operations needed for a given task, he cannot learn to perform it.

The Skinnerian recognizes that the individual does not respond to all available stimuli, and that he may respond in one way on one occasion and in another way on another occasion. The Skinnerian rephrases the issue this way: What are the discriminative stimuli that govern whether a given set of responses will occur or whether a given set of stimuli will be responded to? And how can one bring the child's behavior under the control of an appropriate discriminative stimulus so that he will make sensible "choices" among various possible alternative responses? Bushell says:

> The advantage of the "discriminative stimulus" notion, I think, is that it prescribes a particular course of action when it is observed that a child does not have structures or operations needed for a given task. You don't have to sit around and wring your hands over the fact that a child is not "ready," you go right ahead and shape up the critical stimulus to become an SD for the appropriate response.

The Piagetian is, of course, also interested in how the child acquires the appropriate structures and operations, which he believes determine what a child will select and how he will process a given stimulus input. Opponents of Piaget's theory often claim that the theory is entirely maturational—that it allows for no means by which the needed structures and operations can be taught, so that educators must simply wait for these to unfold spontaneously before they can be used in teaching the child. Some Piagetians may believe this, but the Follow-Through program directors who consider themselves Piagetians do not. They use the theory for their work as follows: Learning is (or should be) more than just "acquiring a response." There is a difference between learning by rote and learning with understanding. If a child is to learn with understanding, he must relate new materials to what he already knows; if there are contradictions between new experiences and old conceptions, he must work to resolve these, and integrate the two. The distinction being made here is akin to one made by the psycholinguists. They distinguish between being able to parrot what someone else has said, and being able to understand and use it in the sense of being able to carry out an action based upon it (follow directions), or generate novel sentences expressing the same thought.

The notion, shared by all programs, that one must start from the child's level at the point of entry into the program is interpreted by the Piagetian to mean that one must find out what "stage" he is in. One can take it for granted that no kindergarten or first-grade child will be capable of the kinds of thinking that characterize the later stage of formal operations. But children from deprived backgrounds may not even have completed the transition from the sensory-motor stage into the pre-operational stage, while most advantaged children will have done so. To the extent that children are still in the earlier stage, Piagetians believe that materials must be so presented that the child can assimilate them in a sensory-motor way. One does not just show a square and tell the child it is a square; one has him trace it with a finger, or walk around a large square on the floor.

From this theoretical standpoint, the sequencing of tasks becomes crucially important. For example, the Piagetian holds that the child cannot understand specific gravity until he has mastered conservation of volume. Conservation of volume, in its turn, depends upon conservation of mass,† which cannot be understood until the child can pay attention to more than one perceptual dimension at one time, and so on. One presents tasks in such an order that the constructs and operations needed for a new task will already have been largely mastered, and one asks about any new task whether the child is "ready" to learn it.

The main Piagetian "stages" refer to some of the major changes in modes of thought that are believed to occur with intellectual development; within these there are smaller sequences—"mini-stages"—and teaching must be paced to these as well. In the teaching of any specific task, or in offering toys for play, the program with a Piagetian bias will try to move the child along through a series of stages by changing the mode of presentation of materials as the child progresses. Both Weikart and Gordon, who have drawn heavily from Piaget's theories in developing their own programs, speak of training their teachers to do this. Weikart gives an illustration:

We try to get the teachers to help think of ways of programing the

---

† "Conservation of mass," in the Piagetian lexicon, refers to the fact that the amount of a substance remains unchanged through a variety of deformations. A ball of plasticine does not become more or less when it is squashed flat, nor does a quantity of water become greater when it is poured into a taller, thinner glass.

tasks. If a child doesn't learn, we say that it is the program that is at fault and go back to a simpler level.

(What do you mean by a simpler level?)

Well, the simplest is the concrete-motoric. Second: representation —have things stand for things. The third is symbolic. Finally, you get signs—words standing for things without any representation. We try to move children along by changing the level at which they pretend. At first, our children play boat by having a real, life-sized boat to get into. Later, they can play with a toy-sized boat, but one that looks like a real boat—isn't too much stylized. Later they can use an ash tray as though it were a boat. We put each child into this sequence, and try to start with toys at the right level of abstraction for the child. We find it's very hard to get the teachers to use the motoric level.

As an aside, it might be worth noting here that some people who find the cognitive-developmental framework congenial as an approach nevertheless find Piaget's work not nearly specific enough when it comes to actually arranging tasks according to the level of cognitive maturity the tasks probably demand. Gordon points out that Piaget's theory lumps all the years from two to seven into one period and gives little detail concerning the transitions that are going on within it.

Resnick, while generally holding more of a reinforcement than a cognitive-developmental viewpoint, also feels there is something to the notion of sensory-motor "readiness":

The general class of perceptual-motor skills are not prerequisites in the sense that you couldn't learn math unless you were good at hopping, but rather in the sense that intellectual learning will be easier if your visual and auditory skills are well developed. That's a hypothesis that we're investing heavily in right now, mainly in a practical sense, developing a real curriculum in that area. The feedback from the kids is so positive. They love this stuff. They feel very successful at it, and perhaps it's mediating their later learning simply by making them be successful.

When the child is in the process of learning something with understanding, he is being very active. He is checking incoming information with his existing concepts, noting contradictions and seeking new information that will help him to resolve conflicts. Indeed, the Piagetian believes, this is how the child changes his internal structures and makes the transition from one stage to the next. The learning situation should be such as to permit him to do this: It should encourage him to ask his own questions and should provide him with materials and questions from a teacher that will illustrate the inadequacies of his preexisting concepts.

"Discovery" and Learning with Understanding ✳

There is an emphasis in some programs on the importance of "discovery." From this point of view, learning is more lasting, or more complete, if the child finds the solution to a problem himself than it is if he is offered a ready-made solution. Nimnicht, whose program attempts to create what he calls a "responsive" learning environment, says:

> Our guiding principle is that the environment should be arranged so that the child is likely to make discoveries about his physical and social world. [It] is based upon the principle that a child better remembers what he discovers for himself. Furthermore, we believe that problem solving is the essence of learning, and is best learned in an environment that poses problems and encourages the discovery of their solutions.
>
> When we say that learning activities should be self-rewarding, we do not mean to imply that a child should never receive praise. But the essential satisfaction should come from the activity and not from something not built into the experience itself.

If one believes that learning occurs only in those moments when the child is actively seeking for something related to his own preestablished concepts and operations, then the job of the educator becomes one of identifying what materials and tasks will fit the child's needs. He takes advantage of any spontaneous search process the child engages in and tries to provide an appropriate response either from materials or from people.

Zimiles stresses how child's play is employed in this way at Bank Street:

> In our program for young children there's a central use of play, and it reflects how the child perceives relationships, reveals how he orders the world, and this is the way he learns to integrate his ideas and to develop them. The task of the teacher in relation to play is to advance it, to make it more coherent, and extend the child's level of functioning. During the preschool year, the child's play shifts to take on a quality of industry and self-initiated activities. He is becoming more involved in understanding the physical and social environment. When the child enters primary school, the teacher's role continues to be one of developing, clarifying, and extending the child's competence, but her techniques for supporting learning through play are different in primary school from what they are in preschool.

In addition to responding to the child's spontaneously initiated activities, including play, the teacher also tries to find ways and means of stimulating the child to start searching. It is these methods and assumptions, as we understand them, that underlie Nimnicht's "autotelic" approach to teaching and learning.

In the Tucson program, Henderson and Hughes emphasize the importance of taking advantage of what the child already knows and of providing teaching materials that fit the child's previous life experiences in some detail. Hughes says:

> With our goals being these intellectual processes: comparing, recalling, looking, consequences, relationships—any content is all right with us. I'm not saying there might not be criteria for content later on. But for the young child, if we're going to build a motivational system for learning and the self-concept "I can learn," we must make the content relevant, give the experiences that evoke this wide range of mental processes, that evoke reorganization, that evoke expansion of what they know, evoke active work on their part.

In this program the teachers find opportunities to teach concepts of proportion, or conjunction, in classroom projects (such as making beef stew) that call for the combination of materials. They take advantage of the sound of a passing fire engine to start a sequential game that involves organizing a hook-and-ladder team and preparing a first-aid station, with the emphasis on relationships among events. Along this line, a Bank Street teacher says:

> Whatever activity is going on, you elicit from it the learning that you can. For instance, if you're working with dough, there are about a million things you can be teaching. Everybody's conversing about it, and what you're conversing about can be size, long, short, sticky, stretching—concepts and vocabulary. Or, you can focus on process, like "How did you get that hole?"

Henderson says about the Tucson reading program:

> When we are trying to teach reading, we try to make it functional; it must be related to experiences the child and his friends have had, it must be useful to the child to be able to read the labels so he can tell what is available where—so he can get the things he wants. We make a lot of use of the primer typewriter to label everything, and then use the labels in referring to materials, places, etc. The better teachers can use this environment easily. Our assumption is that the children are less motivated if you use a more formal program to unlock the recurring environment.

Henderson and Hughes think "relevance" in this sense is the key to "learning with understanding."

In the EDC program there is also a strong emphasis on embedding learning in spontaneously developing life experiences. Armington says:

> We are as concerned with cognitive development as any of the sponsors in the Follow-Through programs. But we resist the idea that cognition can be neatly separated out as just a set of experiences to put children through with the idea of developing certain specified intellectual skills. This is not to rule out the use of exercises from time to time. But in the kind of ongoing, vital life situation that we

know is possible with children, there is all kinds of conceptual development going on even though it's not explicitly planned for. You don't need to sit children down and give them exercises in picking out likenesses and differences. I'm not saying that such games shouldn't be available. Sure they should. But children are doing this all the time in naturalistic ways—whether they're collecting leaves and sorting them out and writing about them in their books, or whether they're looking at beetles and frogs.

What does a behavior modifier have to say about discovery and learning with understanding? Some of the cognitive-developmentalists think that Skinnerians fail to distinguish between rote learning and learning with understanding. Judging from what we have learned in our interviews, this stereotype is false. However, the behavior modifier does insist on a precise definition of what is meant by "learning with understanding" and wants a means by which one can tell whether it has occurred. He believes that "learning with understanding" means being able to generalize correctly to a new instance of a concept. If a concept has been properly taught, the child will have learned to discriminate the relevant dimension and will know the criteria for the inclusion of a new event as an instance of the concept. A concept is thought of as a "set"; it must be taught in such a way as to vary the defining attribute of the set independently of other attributes with which it might be confused.

Engelmann emphasizes that in teaching a concept the teacher must present negative instances as well as positive ones, and he builds the teaching of "not" into the E-B program. Thus, Engelmann holds, if the child is to learn the concept "doll," he must be shown large dolls, small dolls, brown dolls, white dolls, boy dolls, and girl dolls, and told that they are all dolls. Furthermore, he must be shown things that are *not* dolls. In this way he will come to know the defining attributes of the set.

A crucial point for the Skinnerians is that it is not sufficient simply to present the stimuli that the child is to discriminate as being members or not members of a set. The child must be brought to make the correct response in the presence of these stimuli and prevented from making the wrong response. Once the correct response has been made, as Becker says, "You can do something with it." That is, it is available to be strengthened through reinforcement.

For at least some of the Piagetians, however, this is not enough. A young child cannot fully learn a concept unless he has somehow woven it into his own action system. Gordon puts it this way:

> A child learns a concept by a variety of experiences, manipulating a whole set of things around that concept rather than just by being taught "this is a doll, this is a boy." He's got to give you a doll, throw a doll, kiss a doll, take it apart, to really understand this concept.

Teaching and Learning Language ✳

Virtually all the Follow-Through sponsors have placed particular emphasis in their curricula on language acquisition and the skills of literacy—reading and writing. Success in school depends heavily on linguistic fluency, and it is particularly in language that poor children fall short. Different reasons are given: Some say they lack a command of standard English; others say they cannot use language, any language, for abstract reasoning. The sponsors' different views on the nature of learning are further elaborated and exemplified in the different approaches they have taken with respect to teaching language and fostering its development.

Behavior modifiers maintain that if language is to become a salient stimulus for the child, one that he notices and responds to, then the things other people say to him must have consistent consequences for him. This point of view has clear implications for teaching methods. For example, Engelmann and Becker, of the E-B program, argue that simply modeling language for the child is not enough to produce the desired learning. Engelmann notes:

> In other programs they say, "When we walk up the stairs, we say to the children, 'We are walking up the stairs,' " and so forth. The real

test is this: Does the kid have to walk from the signal, or can he just walk up the stairs and ignore what you're saying? No. If you teach the kids that way, they will not be taught.

(Perhaps in other programs they would say that the children will pay attention to language whether it is a signal for their own action or not, just because they want to know what things are called.)

That's like saying, while a child is working on a puzzle, "See that hat on the man?" You have no fix at all that he has any reason for attending to what you say; you're giving him every reason in the world to treat your language as pure noise, because it is in no way related to his outcome.

Reinforcement, then (at least in this instance), is seen as a means of giving a child a reason to attend to the stimuli and to make the relevant response.

Other programs take a great variety of approaches to the teaching of language. Some attempt to "surround the child with language." At Bank Street verbal interaction between the teacher and the child is seen as part of the total process of enabling children to understand the meaning of their experiences and to modify and integrate their perceptions. The teacher encourages the children to talk about their feelings, their concerns, their ideas, partly so she can adapt her own approach to the child to these feelings and ideas; but she also talks to the child about feelings in general and the situations that arouse them, and tries to get the child to talk about these things, on the assumption that this verbalization helps the child to cope with such situations constructively. A Bank Street teacher offers an illustration:

> Let's say ten visitors walk into the room. I'd say to somebody who looks sort of anxious about it that there [are] a lot of visitors here. Then at the same time I'm talking about it and helping him to feel comfortable with it—maybe I'm just putting my arm around the child, or maybe helping him to talk about it. I'm constantly talking about what the children themselves are doing. I'll point out, "Look, you're making a big bubble."

Nimnicht also sees the role of teacher as one of providing verbal mediation for the child:

I do not feel that a child in downtown Oakland is not getting a lot of sensory experience; he is getting more than he needs. What you come down to is that it is undifferentiated, probably not understood; he is not getting interpreted data. We feel we must clean up the environment somewhat—not overwhelm his senses with "things" all over the classroom—clean it up and reduce the number of things that are happening so that he can focus on something—can see or hear something without distraction. The second implication is that you do not just put him in a rich environment and expect good things to happen because he is now getting sensory experience. It has to be interpreted; there has to be someone providing verbal mediation for him to understand what he is seeing and perceiving.

Nimnicht trains his teachers to avoid "irrelevant" verbalization and to concentrate their verbal fire on the dimensions of the task that they want the child to learn. The teacher might hold up two color chips and say, "Which one is the green one?" If the child chooses the blue one, the teacher says, "That is the blue one; which is the green one?" She does not say, "You were wrong," but provides another occasion to give the right response.

The Tucson program, which places heavy emphasis on language training, also avoids correction while nevertheless giving extensive feedback. Henderson describes the procedures as follows:

We use a very well-specified method of interaction between children and teachers. It doesn't involve just talking to the children, which is what teachers have been doing for a long time. The teachers are taught to interact verbally with children in order to get the children to communicate. She reinforces all attempts of the child to communicate. If he wants to speak in Spanish, that's fine. The teacher builds on the responses that the child offers, responds to the idea presented, and expands the child's utterances.

Here is a sample of a dialogue between a Tucson teacher and a group of children at the zoo:

"He scratching herself," said Alfred.
"That's him house," commented Juan.

"He's eating with he hands," continued Gloria.
Teacher: "The monkey's hands are paws, he's eating with his paws."†

In this instance the teacher was modeling correct syntax as well as offering a more semantically correct word, without telling the children that their initial phrases had been incorrect.

The Mexican-American children in the Tucson program tend to be silent, at least in a school setting. It is especially difficult to get language *production* (as distinct from understanding) from them. This is one of the reasons for not telling the child he is wrong when he makes a mistake—this tends to drive him back into silence. Positive reinforcement is used, however.

At Tucson the effort to teach word mastery involves an intimate interaction between the child's speaking, the teacher's speaking, and the sight of the printed word. Hughes says:

> We are trying to lead the child into the process of reading through recording his own utterances, showing what it looks like, then reading it back to him. This activity takes place most frequently in a one-to-one relationship and is accompanied by a statement of reinforcement, such as, "You used an interesting word to tell how you felt," "You saw so much," or "I wanted to write it down." It is but a short time until most children are asking to have what they say written down. Soon children's statements are organized around some shared experiences: a trip, cooking, visitor, etc. These records become books or talking murals.

Gotkin also notes the importance of getting the child to produce language and believes that this is one of the advantages of his games approach:

> Normally, teachers don't necessarily teach the kids to produce the names of objects. They'll say, "Find me the tambourine," and the kid will get it. Then the teacher asks, "What is that?" and the kid won't produce the word. The instructional events don't require the

† Arline Hobson, "Systematic Language Modeling," *Contemporary Education,* Vol. XL, No. 4 (1969), pp. 225–27.

production of language. That's what I'm trying to do with the games. The reason I like games is that it's a social situation. It's very easy for kids to become leaders, so they are learning not just the content of the game, but to use language to give instructions. They are not just respondents.

In Weikart's program, teachers verbalize extensively and try to get reciprocal verbalizations from the child:

> We ask the teachers to give the children practice in labels, and also [to] emphasize the relational words "same as," "third," and so on. We find that the teachers tend to simplify their language too much— they'll say, "Get in line," and we want them to say, "*If* everyone is quiet, *then* we will get in line." We ask the teachers to present choices verbally: "There are two ways we can go to the coat closet —straight across the room or around the table by the wall. Which way shall we go?" We ask them to avoid giving directions with body English. We tell the child what he's doing while he's doing it, and ask him to tell us what he's doing. We might even stop a child when he's halfway down a slide and ask him what he's doing. Then we tell him what he's done, and what he's going to do, and get him to produce these constructions before we move on to the next step.

These excerpts seem to indicate that nobody in Follow-Through simply talks to the child about whatever comes into his head in the hope that this will stimulate language development. Everyone recognizes that a child will not learn the meaning of words or grammatical structures unless he attends to the words themselves while he is attending to the stimuli (and attributes of stimuli, or relationships among stimuli) that the words are meant to refer to. Finally, everyone takes it as a goal that the child should be able to produce appropriate words and phrases, as well as to understand them. The differences among programs seem to lie in what procedures are thought to bring these conditions about, and in what detail they are specified. Some programs assume that if the teacher achieves a close match between what she says and what the child is doing, this will be sufficient to ensure that the child will attend to what she says. Others argue that the teacher's

verbalization must be in response to something the child has said
or done—an answer to his question or an expansion of his spontaneous verbalization. In a Skinnerian program the necessary
element is that there shall be some desirable consequence for the
child in his attending to, understanding, and using language.

The Importance of Sequencing Tasks ✳

Both the behavior modifier and the cognitive-developmentalist
recognize the importance of sequencing. Although the behavior
modifier does not conceive of sequencing in terms of a universal set
of "stages," as does the cognitive-developmentalist, he does recognize that certain operations are contingent upon being able to do
other operations. Thus, the child cannot learn to read a new word
with understanding (that is, identify its referent) unless he has
previously learned a set of letter-sound correspondences. Similarly,
he cannot do long division until he has mastered multiplication.
In the E-B program, for example, Engelmann and Becker teach
the meaning of the "equal" sign in arithmetical addition by the
use of a balance around a fulcrum. Their purpose is to establish
a base for later generalization of arithmetical operations to algebra.
The usual methods of teaching addition and subtraction, which rely
on rote learning, produce little transfer when the child arrives at
algebra; he feels he is encountering something brand new. This
need not be the case if the concept of "equals" is taught, in the first
place, over the full set of instances to which it should apply.

Clearly, if one is to teach certain skills, one must analyze
what skills (if any) they depend on and teach these first. The importance of sequencing is not, then, a real point of difference between the two schools of thought. There is, however, a difference
in what the necessary sequences are thought to be. The Piagetian
thinks in fairly global terms about the total organization of thought
processes and believes that preexisting structures operate as a
constraint upon the acquisition of specific bits of knowledge or
specific skills. The Skinnerian tends to deal with narrower, much
more specific skills. In defining the sequencing of tasks, the Piaget-

ian tends to equate "usual" or "normative" with "necessary." That is, if on the average most children do not acquire conservation of volume until several years after they have acquired conservation of substance, the conservation of substance is assumed to be a necessary but not sufficient condition for understanding the conservation of volume. The Skinnerian asserts, however, that the usual sequence need *not* imply a functional dependence of one thing on the other and therefore will not restrict himself to the Piagetian descriptions in deciding what the right sequencing for teaching is. Furthermore, the Skinnerian believes the acquisition of a physical concept can proceed through the learning of an abstract rule; the Piagetian believes such learning must involve interaction with the physical world.

The difference in point of view is illustrated in fascinating detail in a recent passage of arms between Engelmann and Constance Kamii, a Piagetian. Engelmann has argued that Piaget's theory has no application to teaching, except to point out certain skills that children are normally not taught. He argues that children young enough so that they would normally be in the "preoperational" stage can be taught logical processes that normally do not occur until much later (the stage of "formal operations"). To prove his point he set out to teach the concept of specific gravity to a group of kindergarten children who had just reached the age of six. He taught the children a rule about why some things float and others don't: Something will float in water if it is "lighter than a piece of water the same size." He felt that he had succeeded in teaching this concept to the children so that they understood it and were able to apply it to new instances. He agreed to have Dr. Kamii come to his lab and test a group of the children—four in number—with any tests she wished to devise. It is not possible to present the results in detail here.† Like most "crucial" experiments, this one had ambiguous results. Kamii concluded that the children's understanding of the concept was partial at best, that

---

† C. Kamii and L. Derman, "The Engelmann Approach to Teaching Logical Thinking: Findings from the Administration of Some Piagetian Tasks," in D. R. Green, M. P. Ford, and G. Flamer, eds., *Piaget and Measurement* (New York: McGraw-Hill, in press).

they still showed a good deal of "pre-operational" thinking, and that they frequently applied their rule in a rote fashion. Engelmann's view was that this seemed to be the case only because the children did not have the information that would have been necessary for them to use the rule with understanding, and that when they did have this information, they used the rule with all the sophistication that normally characterizes older children.

Let us examine some of the children's responses, to make it clearer how these differences in interpretation could arise. First of all, when an object was put into water, the children would recite the rule correctly when asked to explain why it had sunk or floated. When the large, heavy ball bearing was put into mercury and it floated, the children were surprised, but said that this occurred because it was lighter than a piece of *mercury* the same size. Thus, they were able to generalize the rule to a new medium. But when asked to predict whether a piece of soap would float if it were put into mercury, they thought it would sink—thus revealing that they had not mastered the seriation aspects of the problem. Dr. Kamii presented the children with a number of objects—a paper clip, pieces of soap of various sizes, a metal plate, ball bearings of various sizes, a needle, and candles of two sizes. She then asked the children to put them into two piles—the things that would float in water and the things that would not. They classified objects according to a number of sometimes inconsistent principles, just as a group of untrained children their own age would normally do. They might as well have been with Piaget in Geneva. They said a paper clip would sink because it had little hooks on it that would pull it down into the water. They said the needle would sink because it was thin, or would float because it was lightweight. They did not pick up the needle and say, "Well, this is so small, a piece of water this size wouldn't weigh very much." The small candle would float because it was small; the large candle would sink because it was large and therefore "heavy." In other words, when asked to *predict* about floating or sinking, they did not make use of their rule. and they reasoned "pre-operationally."

Engelmann argued that this occurred because the children had no knowledge about the materials things were made of, and whether the material was homogeneous throughout an object or from one instance of a class to another. Specifically, how would they know that the big candle was made of the same material as the small one? The proper test, Engelmann insisted, would involve cutting a candle into two unequal pieces, putting one portion into water, and asking the child to predict what the other portion would do. When the test was performed in this way, the children passed it. So it would appear that at least part of their difficulty in prediction did stem from the lack of an item of relevant information. It is interesting that during the Kamii prediction test, the children never asked for the information they needed—they never asked whether the large and small candles were made out of the same stuff, or whether candle wax weighs more or less than water—they simply regressed to a less mature mode of thought.

The proper interpretation of this experiment will be argued for a long time to come. It does point up several of the relevant issues about readiness and sequencing. Engelmann's children did achieve a level of competence on this task that was beyond what an orthodox Piagetian would consider possible at this age. This fact suggests that attempts to teach should not be limited by current concepts of what a child's capacities at a given stage are. However, there are some sobering provisos. First of all, if one attempts to teach a child something that is more complex and sophisticated than most of his existing concepts and skills, one is likely to be tripped up by the child's lack of some knowledge or skill that one had not realized in advance was necessary for the task. Secondly, one may find that the younger child lacks the necessary information-gathering strategies for determining exactly when and how his learned principle applies to a new situation. He does not operate in a hypothesis-testing manner. No doubt, Engelmann would say that this strategy, too, is something that can be taught, and it would be very enlightening to see what success one would have in attempting to do this. In any case, its absence in the normal young child (whether advantaged or disadvantaged) imposes a limitation on the uses to which a child can put an advanced concept. Beyond this, there is the question of retention. If one teaches something that cannot be integrated easily into the body of knowledge and skills the child already has, will it be quickly forgotten? If it turns out with further experimentation that an advanced concept continues to be remembered and used by a young child who learned it "too early" (by the Piagetian's reckoning), then one can begin to forget about teaching only the concepts that are appropriate to the child's level of development. There is a further point about retention: Suppose a child "learns" an advanced concept that he can use in some situations but cannot always generalize from correctly; and suppose he retains the concept for a brief time and then loses it. It may still be that the learning was worth something, in making the child "readier" for the next try at this or another task.

A number of people have pointed out that we lack good experimental evidence concerning what skills and knowledge are necessary for the acquisition of other skills and knowledge; this being the case, they argue, a good pragmatic rule is this: When in doubt whether a child is "ready" to learn something, try to teach it to him and find out! Becker underlines this point:

There is one basic assumption underlying our thinking: If you want to know what you can teach a child, try it. We've made no assumptions on the basis of any labels that you can place on kids, or tests you can give kids, as to what can be taught. We consider this useless information for the most part. Generally, we've been pleased with the results of this approach. It is empirical, rather than making unnecessary generalizations from inadequate research.

The point is also made that, the merits of optimal sequencing aside, a "developmental" or "readiness" point of view tends to discourage efforts to teach children who are not learning easily. In the controversy over learning the concept of specific gravity, the developmentalist gets his satisfaction—his point of view is sustained—if the younger children *fail* to learn something. The reinforcement learning theorist wants to prove that the younger children *can* learn something quite difficult. These facts may imply something about the amount of effort the proponents of each camp are willing to put into teaching. Engelmann makes a related point:

There are all kinds of safe hypotheses we can make about kids. We're really making statements about the probabilities of what [already] has been taught in their environment. Let's say we establish some cognitive criteria for reading readiness. They'll usually be some rather sophisticated discriminations. We find that if we assemble kids who don't meet these criteria (and teach them properly), not one in a hundred would fail to learn to read. You can use teaching methods that are really quite poor and they learn to read [in no time at all].

We can define reading readiness as a broad spectrum of skills, and then we'll find that any environment that has taught a kid this skill and this skill and this skill has also taught him everything that's relevant for reading. [If you only try to teach the kids that have these skills] it's a pure and simple cop-out. I can tell you what kids need in order to be able to read, and we can teach that.

Another comment on this point is this: "If you confine your reading training to the kids who pass a 'reading readiness' test, you're just helping the rich get richer."

In point of fact, programs stemming from radically different theoretical points of view seem to have made very similar judgments concerning what it is appropriate to try to teach during the first year of a Follow-Through program. Everybody is working on relational concepts such as "between," "under," "more and less." Engelmann and Becker are not spending much time trying to teach specific gravity. The actual content of their program is pretty much what a cognitive-developmental theory would specify as suitable for this age range.

Some programs do not fall clearly into either the Piagetian or the Skinnerian camps with regard to the sequencing of tasks. The point of view of Hughes and Henderson's Tucson program is that a wide variety of possible sequences will work and that the important thing is to try to "embed" or "integrate" new items into what the child already knows and is interested in. Henderson puts it this way:

My own feeling is that there is no single best series of experiences for the teaching of concepts to all children. If we are working toward generalization or transfer of concepts, we probably need to provide a broad range of exemplars of concepts, as they are present in many materials and as functionally equivalent skills may be exercised in many contexts. Generalization may be especially facilitated when concepts are learned in a range of situations which are relevant to the child's own life. One assumption of our program is that it is not necessary to prescribe a single sequence of experiences for each concept to be learned.

The Bank Street approach also emphasizes the need to recognize the individual child's framework of knowledge and his preferred media of learning, in order to maximize the probability that his learning will involve integration and understanding. The program strives for multiple exposures of a concept through a variety of media, so as to make learning personally meaningful and to achieve generality. The multiplicity is thought to be more important than the order in which the exposures occur.

Resnick's program, in contrast, is committed to the empirical discovery of optimal sequences:

> We define some behaviors that we want to produce in children. We define the situation we want as an end result. We analyze these terminal objectives, and derive a set of hypotheses concerning the order in which behaviors are acquired. That is, we have a sequence of behaviors and a rough hypothesis that this is an optimal order for acquiring them. We're not committed to that order in any rigid way. We then construct a test for every item in the sequence. By test, I mean something terribly simple. If you want to know whether a child can perform a behavior, you set up a situation in which he can perform it, and watch. Test theorists call these "criterion referenced tests."

Frequent testing in the Resnick program reveals how difficult each individual task is. The order of tasks is then readjusted on the basis of this information. Resnick has found, for example, that color concepts are more difficult to master than shape concepts, and therefore plans to move training in color naming and color sorting to a later point in the curriculum. Even among tasks of similar difficulty there may be optimal orders, and Resnick is embarking on a series of experimental studies of variations in order of tasks to discover what some of the optimal orders are.

The distinction we have drawn between "behavior modification" and "developmental" approaches admittedly oversimplifies theoretical differences among the programs. There has been an infusion of ideas from the field of programed instruction, growing out of work on computer simulation and information processing. Gotkin's games program reflects the influence of these sources. He finds two main advantages in the programed instruction approach: It calls for very clear specification of instructional objectives, and it requires the teacher to plan in detail how tasks are to be presented and in what order. Gotkin reports that with only a few hours of instruction, it has been possible to get five-year-olds to read trigrams (CAT, BIT, RAG), provided the learning steps are properly sequenced from simple to complex. An important principle of his approach is that successive tasks proceed to more complex levels in small steps, with the objective of letting the child go through the series without making errors.

As we have seen, many teachers and program directors stress the importance of getting the child to make the right response and urge that if errors occur, learning has been actively retarded. To overstate the case somewhat, the argument is that children do *not* learn from their mistakes and should be prevented from making them. We noted earlier that a number of programs have found it undesirable to give negative corrective feedback—to say "that was wrong" when the child makes a mistake. Usually this practice is rejected because of its motivational consequence. It is thought to make the child afraid of failure, or at least to make him less interested in the task. Nevertheless, it is generally agreed that there must be feedback of some sort that permits the child to know whether he is on the right track. The solution, according to Gotkin and others, is to program the learning steps cleverly enough so that the child will be able to succeed on each new item and will therefore get only positive feedback.

As we noted earlier, the Skinnerian stresses the importance of devices to elicit the correct response, because it is only when this response (or one approximating it) has occurred that reinforcement can be brought to bear. Learning theorists who do not depend upon reinforcement, but only upon the contiguous occurrence of a response in the presence of the cues that are to control it, also must employ all their skill to get the correct response to occur. Active participation by the learner is of the essence for such theorists,† and so is the prevention of errors. When a student makes a wrong response, according to contiguity learning theory, he is not only failing to learn the correct response, but he is actively learning something else that will interfere with correct learning and that will have to be unlearned. Although Gotkin does not explicitly rely on contiguity learning theory, it seems to be implicit in many of the procedures that he uses, such as "language lotto" and a variety of matrix games. He finds that these games get a higher level of active participation, and that they can also be sequenced in small steps so as to increase the probability of errorless performance. Also, negative feedback can be avoided. Gotkin says:

> The value of using a structured set of games is that the kids master the rules of the game, and once they've got that you keep adding new materials and then they become very fast learners. The structure is in the rules and in the materials. What we're after is interactional rules. The interaction between the kids is gamelike. You're correcting without ever saying "No" to the child.

Gotkin does point out the great practical difficulty of devising series that are sufficiently well-tailored to the pace and skills of each child. With the programing time available to most classrooms, most programs cannot offer enough branching for maximum individual effectiveness. Nevertheless, sequences can be identified that suit a reasonably high proportion of children for many content series.

The Emotional Aspects of Learning ✳

The discussion so far has not done justice to the distinctions among programs that have to do with how the child's learning relates to emotional development. The British Infant Schools and Bank

---

† A. A. Lumsdaine and Robert Glasser, *Teaching Machines and Programmed Learning: A Source Book* (Washington, D.C.: National Education Association, 1960).

Street, for example, emphasize the affectional relationships between the child and the teacher far more than either an exclusively Piaget-based or a behavior modification program. In part, this relationship is thought to be important because of its bearing upon the child's willingness to learn; but in some programs the establishment of social relationships and social competence is also thought to be important in its own right—as important as the acquisition of cognitive contents. Gotkin says about the use of games as a teaching method:

> Our kids are learning social skills as well. If there's anything about ghetto life, it's that the kids have been underlings. Their parents have been underlings, and then the kids have been underlings. I'm interested in Child Power—that the kid should be learning to manage himself.

Charles Ascheim, of the EDC program, makes a similar point in describing EDC:

> Cognitive growth is perhaps a minor and certainly only one part of all of the growth that you're interested in.
> (What might be equally or more important?)
> The growth of a kid's ability to live in a society with other human beings in mutually productive, growing ways.

Furthermore, emotional reactions are thought to be inseparable from intellectual operations. Armington says:

> One's cognitive life is not separated from one's affective life. Thought and emotion can't be separated. People tend to think of a concept as something you have or don't have. Actually, it's not just a question of what you know, but how you feel about it, how you relate to the concept. You can know it, or do it, as something you enjoy, or something you feel you can learn how to do. What is a child's concept of mathematics, or a point in mathematics? What is his concept of reading? It involves more than just knowledge.

In a similar vein, Bank Street regards the acquisition of academic skills as only one facet of the learning that takes place in school. Zimiles makes this comment:

> The school's prime concern should be directed toward improving the child's image of himself as a learner. This calls for the fostering of an attitude of openness and receptivity and the development of powers of concentration. The entire school environment must be directed toward providing clarity, meaningfulness, and gratification, so that learning at all levels may be facilitated.

At Bank Street intellectual development is thought to be intimately related to impulse expression and the growth of impulse control. In a paper stating some of the assumptions underlying the Bank Street program, Edna Shapiro says:

> Growth and maturing involve conflict. The inner life of the growing child is a play of forces between urgent drives and impulses, contradictory impulses within the self, and demanding reality outside the self. The resolution of these conflicts bears the imprint of the quality of the interaction with the salient life figures and the demands of the culture.
>
> Thus, . . . the inner emotional and impulse life of the child is seen as inextricably part of his growth and development; both affective and cognitive development are considered to be shaped by the nature of the individual's encounters with the environment.†

The emotional aspects of learning are intimately related to the problem of motivation, which we shall discuss in the next chapter. As we shall see, some programs have a goal that goes considerably beyond academic objectives. They would like to help the children in their care to become autonomous individuals in all aspects of their lives, even extending to them the freedom *not* to acquire certain aspects of traditional academic skills.

---

† Edna Shapiro, "The Developmental-Interaction Approach to the Education of Young Children" (November, 1969), a working paper of the Research Division, Bank Street College of Education, 216 West 14 Street, New York, N.Y.

4*

Motivation and Incentives

It is in their views about motivation and its role in learning that the most profound differences among the programs are found. No one doubts that children must be interested in what they are doing if they are to be effectively taught. The issues lie in how this interest is best aroused and maintained. And views about motivation are closely linked with educational objectives. Some programs are oriented toward teaching their children a given body of knowledge and skills, while others consider it their basic task to make children into autonomous learners. These different objectives seem to dictate reliance on different motivational systems. We first present, in some detail, a few views about motivation, and then attempt to identify some of the assumptions that underlie these views and their implications for educational practice. We might simply note in passing that the issues we are discussing represent some very old problems in modern dress. They go back at least to Locke and Rousseau. At present these issues are by no means confined to Head Start and Follow-Through programs—they are at the heart of arguments about "progressive," "permissive," and "traditional" education.

Intrinsic Motivation ✳

Not surprisingly, cognitive-developmentalists and behavior modifiers differ with respect to motivation as well as the other issues already discussed. Cognitive-developmental theory holds that mastery of new tasks is intrinsically gratifying to the child. If one presents the child with something too easy—already mastered—he will be bored and lose interest. If it is just slightly above his present level of functioning, his interest will be engaged, and he will work on it without needing extrinsic incentives. This "work" involves, as Weikart puts it, the child's "creation of representations of himself and his environment." We presume Weikart, as a Piagetian, would want to add the reorganization of previously acquired representations as part of what goes on in learning. If the task calls for previously acquired concepts and operations (or representations) that are considerably more complex than the ones the child has already developed, he will again not engage himself with the task, and no learning will occur.

There is also a good deal of emphasis on intrinsic motivation by people who emphasize social-emotional factors in learning. The Bank Street point of view, for example, is well expressed by the teacher who says:

> I believe that learning takes place really when children are self-motivated. It doesn't mean you don't introduce things the children have not expressed interest in, because you just can't limit your program to what they already know. You know, as an adult, what the children should be learning or might be interested in, so you'll introduce something. But when you introduce a new thing to even a group of five children, some might be interested in it and some might not, and they'll all be ready for it in different ways and take it in their own particular way. I don't think they're going to learn it just because you introduce it, so there's no point in pushing it.
> (But what happens when the child is not interested and you think it's important?)
> You find another way to teach it. If you're teaching "big" and

"little" and you tried it with one material, you try it another way, when he's out climbing on something: "You're taller than I am," or "I can't reach you because you're higher." When he's really involved you teach him. I really don't believe he's going to learn it otherwise; if he does learn it, it's going to be a very superficial learning and it's not going to stick with him.

Gordon, a Piagetian, makes a related point:

We're really believers in intrinsic motivation—the personal search for meaning rather than in the behavior modification or external reinforcer. No kid ever needs a raisin, an M & M, or what have you, for doing anything; being able to *do* is its own reward.

Armington stresses the importance of placing children in surroundings that will develop their spontaneous interest in learning before attempting to teach specific skills such as reading:

(What do you think there is about the Infant School classroom that makes it easy for children to learn to read?)
By the time the child is ready to crack the code, he has reached a fairly high degree of linguistic development, of speech development. He has acquired, if not a love of books, at least an affinity for the printed word by being surrounded by books and other children who derive pleasure from books, by being in an environment where adults are reading and writing and enjoying that activity. So learning to read is something which he wants very much to do, and for intrinsically valid reasons, and not simply to satisfy a parental expectation.

In the EDC program there is an effort to make learning relevant to what are seen as the child's own needs, rather than to lead the child into wanting what the program directors feel he should want. With this distinction in mind, they distrust the conventional views of "motivation":

ARMINGTON: "Motivation," conventionally conceived, is how do I get the child to do what *I* want him to do. We would say instead, "How do I enable the child to do what *he* needs to do?"

ASCHEIM: All kids have needs. And working them out or working within them is a large part of what growth is about. "Motivation" turns out to describe what you have to do with a kid if his needs don't happen to correspond to what your needs for him are.

ARMINGTON: I think there is nothing more disagreeable to a young child than boredom. It's natural for a young child to be active mentally and physically. What we need to do in school is to capitalize on this natural energy. If the environment is suitably provisioned, and if the teacher is suitably sensitive, there will be vitality in the classroom, and this vitality is contagious from one child to another. So the problem of how to motivate children tends to vanish.

In the EDC program it is not thought to be necessary to provide the child with specific rewards or incentives for specific "correct" responses. We noted earlier that many programs emphasize the importance of feedback to the child that will give him information about his progress in learning, but in the non-Skinnerian programs this feedback is not thought of as "reinforcement," nor is it given to provide incentives for learning. Nimnicht, for example, using some of the theory and engineering of O. K. Moore and his associates, attempts to provide a "responsive environment" in his classrooms, so that the child will be guided in his search for problem solutions by the very materials he is working with. Moore's automated typewriter is designed to give immediate feedback to the child as to whether he has achieved a correct solution. If he has, the machine works. If he does the wrong thing, such as hitting two keys at the same time, the machine turns off. Immediate feedback to the child as to whether he is on the right track toward the solution of a problem is essential to learning, in this view, just as it is in programs based on reinforcement theory. The difference is that in Nimnicht's program, the child is not thought to need an "extrinsic" motivator such as a token or even praise. It should be noted that Nimnicht is not saying that children learn simply from undirected contact with standard play materials. Materials have to be very carefully engineered if they are to get the child to form concepts about the rightness or wrongness of his groupings. Gordon comments on how difficult this is to do and notes that sometimes feedback from the teacher is indispensable:

A language game was given to us by a toy company which wanted feedback on what we thought of it. Our disadvantaged youngsters were very intrigued by all of the motor aspects of it, pushing the lever and watching something go, but they didn't respond to the language cue. The middle-class kid is not so intrigued by the motor aspects, which he sees as a device for getting the machine to talk to him, so he can talk back to it. How are we going to turn that machine into a teaching device? What some of these toys do is simply help the rich get richer. So we have to take something that was designed for middle-class kids mostly, and for the child to do by himself, and convert it into an interpersonal situation between an adult and a child in which this becomes simply the delivery system for what we want to accomplish, and eventually maybe he can go off and fiddle around with it.

(So you do stress an interpersonal situation?)

Very much. This is why I have three adults for five children. We think this is the way kids learn. I guess in a way we're the opposite of computer-assisted instruction. These children don't learn from an object by themselves. They have to have some cuing as to what to do with an object.

A primary objective of Gotkin's games program is that children develop autonomy. Thus it stresses materials that either provide their own feedback or can function with feedback given by a group of children to one another. Gotkin reports that many games that adults try to use for instructional purposes (such as checkers, or even Simon Says) prove too difficult for children without a great deal of help from adults. But there are other games that can be scaled to the appropriate level of difficulty, and when this is done, the children quickly learn to play in groups with very little adult supervision. In a Gotkin classroom, groups of children may be seen selecting their own games to play and teaching any new child (or visiting adult) how to play them. The teacher, of course, helps to reprogram the content available for choice, so that something new and challenging within a familiar format is always available.

In the programs that emphasize intrinsic motivation, the child is thought of as being innately equipped with curiosity or exploratory motivation. This is something that a program can count on; it does not have to be built up through association with other forms of gratification.

Resnick has an interesting comment on curiosity and its function as a motivator:

> I don't think I've ever seen a child who's in a normal intelligence range who was not curious. I've seen many, many children whose curiosity did not organize a sequence of activities for them. There is a difference between the curiosity of a kid who opens a box and looks into everything and the curiosity of a child who can work for five minutes to get the box open. And there are many, many children who enter without the latter. There are almost none who enter without the former. Some of them become scared to express their wish to explore, and that's not too hard to free them of. But it's harder to let the exploratory drive be the reinforcer that organizes a string of activities. And that's what we mean by attention span. And that's what we mean by delayed gratification, and that's what we mean by intrinsic motivation.

External Reinforcement ✳

All the Follow-Through programs use praise and approval in some form. The behavior modifiers, however, make these explicitly contingent on specific behavior. Traditional Skinnerian concepts of motivation are partly embodied in the notion of "setting conditions," such as deprivation or satiation, that help to determine how effective a reinforcer will be at any given time. A hungry animal or child will work (that is, will learn a new task or bit of behavior) to get food. For an overfed animal or child, food is not an effective reinforcer. Reinforcement is linked to motivation in another way: Reinforcers govern the strength (or probability of occurrence) of behavior, and often people referring to "highly motivated behavior" mean simply that it is strongly learned, or highly probable. Although children can be taught to administer reinforcement to themselves, behavior modifiers do not consider any other meaning for the concept "intrinsic motivation" useful. We quote from a joint interview with Engelmann and Becker:

(Some people argue that teaching should occur in response to some signal from the child that he wants to know something.)

ENGELMANN: Why wait? What evidence is there that it's going to destroy a kid, or that it will be any less real, if you first show him that there's a payoff for learning? You say, "Come on over here, I want to teach you something." And you teach him. You can carry the task farther and teach it more efficiently that way. Instead of a sloppy demonstration, why not have something arranged in advance that allows you to teach it faster?

(The argument is that the teaching somehow sticks better, becomes better integrated with whatever else the child knows, if you choose the moment when he wants to learn it.)

ENGELMANN: That means: "When it's easy for me to teach it, that's when I teach it." It also means someone really taught the child at home.

(Do you see any distinction between the so-called intrinsic and extrinsic motivation?)

ENGELMANN: I really don't know what that means—what extrinsic motivation is—that the payoff is built into the task?

(Usually that's what *intrinsic* motivation means—that the payoff is built into the task. If you have to apply something else, or else the child won't do it, that's what most people call *extrinsic*.)

ENGELMANN: Then "intrinsic" just means that there's no payoff, no training. You give a child a task and say he should be intrinsically motivated to do it, but there's no attempt to structure the task so there will be a relevant basis for this intrinsic motivation.

If you want to achieve what you call intrinsic motivation, you have to operate in a way that you'll get it, and you'll never get it unless you show the kid there is some kind of payoff for doing it. What kind of payoff do you get in a typical school situation? We say, "Kid, which would you rather have, the lesser or the greater of two punishments? If you fool around, you get the big punishment— your mother will call the school, and so on. But if you go through all this Mickey Mouse, that's not so bad, you can endure that. Which would you rather choose?"

(We're wondering about what we saw this morning, when the teacher was playing a game with the children and put points up on the board for the children when they won and points for herself when she won: The children had seven points and she had two, and she said, "I won," and they said, "You did not, seven is more than two!" Was there any intrinsic motivation involved in being able to count those numbers correctly?)

ENGELMANN: It's all extrinsic.

(What about being able to read a story that's interesting?)

BECKER: There you build the reinforcers into the plot of the task.

ENGELMANN: It's intrinsic to the task, but not to the child.

(Could you say that the nature of the child is such that these tasks are intrinsically interesting?)

BECKER: There has to be a learning history before they are reinforcing.

ENGELMANN: Give me any kid who's intrinsically motivated and I can edit that out of him in nothing flat. Punish him for doing those behaviors.

(And when you remove the punishment?)

ENGELMANN: If you use effective enough punishment you can probably control it. On the other hand, if you want a kid to persist where he's going to have to work hard before he gets a payoff, you just structure it. You start off with Task A, where there's a little bit of punishment (work), large payoff. Then you start making the "punishment" part bigger and bigger, and pretty soon you get to where you can say, "Listen. This is really hard, and it's going to take you a long time to learn it. You don't have to try." He'll say, "I'll try."

Engelmann and Becker, then, do not deny that the child may want to learn for learning's own sake. They simply say they do not wish to leave it to chance whether this motivation develops. Nor do they feel it necessary to wait for a moment when the child's curiosity is spontaneously aroused before teaching. They say these "intrinsic" motivations are teachable, something that can be deliberately aroused if a teaching situation is properly structured. Becker comments as follows:

If you look at the words people use in the Follow-Through programs about incentives and motivations, you find disparities. If you look at their procedures and actions, you find very little differences, except when precise or good materials or interesting things to do aren't sufficient to bring a child onto a task. Then, in our program, we'll go to something stronger. We aren't left with no alternatives when "intrinsic" incentives don't work. This, to me, is the key difference.

The behavior theorists discuss the kind of motivation that is involved in persisting in a task that is difficult, requires effort, and offers no immediate payoff. They hold that such motivation can be built up by gradually increasing the ratio of effort to reinforcement.

How, exactly, do the people who use behavior modification techniques employ reinforcement in their programs? It has almost universally been found that it is unnecessary to use material rewards such as candy or toys. "Social reinforcement"—praise, approval—seems adequate to produce the desired results. Resnick looks upon the dispensing of social reinforcement as one of the three basic functions of teachers:

We have identified three teacher functions which I believe exist in every Follow-Through classroom, and also in traditional classrooms. There is a function of diagnosing and prescribing for children. There's a tutoring and teaching function, which can be central if you opt for the Engelmann method, or more supplementary if you use the more indirect methods. Either of these functions can be dropped out for a given day or a given week and you don't see any difference in our classrooms. One that cannot be dropped out is the third function, which is the maintenance of on-task behavior. We call it "reinforcement," but we're not dogmatic about what the reinforcer is. The thing is to make sure for every child in your classroom that reinforcers (whatever is reinforcing for *him*) keep coming on a sufficiently dense schedule to keep him working.

We have described a role in the classroom of the "traveling teacher." She moves around on a schedule that simply gets her to all the children frequently. The rule is, when she gets to a child, she should attend to him positively. *How* she does it—that's up to her personal style. She doesn't stay with any child longer than one minute—that's to get her around frequently.

Incidentally, this thing can really change form. One of our teachers sprained her ankle a couple of months ago, and she couldn't move. So she sat down and the kids came to her, and it still worked. So the important thing isn't the physical movement. It's the frequency of contact.

The question is sometimes raised as to whether children are responsive to social reinforcement at the time of their entry into compensatory education programs. Most program directors seem to feel that these children enter with adequately developed social responsiveness. As Resnick puts it:

> The greatest deficit for these children with respect to other children is intellectual. It's also where the greatest competence of the school lies. We can't love the children. First of all, I believe most of them are loved [a lot at home]. Of course, there are some cases of real neglect, but for most of them there is at least as strong an emotional base to work from as in any other social group. Every contact I have had with these parents has reinforced the belief that they are not only skilled but concerned. If that's true, the biggest problem is not in the emotional but in the cognitive area.

Some feel that the deprived child often does have some "deficit" in the emotional area as well, at least as far as his reactions to school personnel are concerned, and that a first task of the program must be to establish responsiveness to the teachers. A comment from Bank Street:

> Trust is a very important thing we found missing in a lot of the children that come into the center. It's especially important for three-year-olds who are first separated from their mother. Usually you become the first other figure to be trusted, but if you have children that don't trust adults to begin with, you've got a much more difficult problem. We've had a lot of acting-out and aggressive children. First and foremost, before you can get to the specifics of the curriculum, your curriculum must be establishing trust, and you establish that through the structure of your program.
> (Do you think they can't learn unless they trust?)
> We've had a lot of children who've really had a hard time concentrating on just playing. They're so busy testing out their relationship with adults that that becomes the first and foremost thing you have

to get to before you get into the specifics of cognitive learning. Except you don't wait; you do both at the same time.

Most programs have found that the children are responsive to praise and approval either upon entry or very soon thereafter and rely upon these forms of teacher response to motivate the children's participation in the teaching-learning process.

The question of what kind of reinforcers to use is handled quite pragmatically in many programs. Bushell dispenses tokens (poker chips), along with praise, to serve as a tangible symbol of the teacher's approval. These chips also serve as material rewards, since they can be exchanged for the chance to participate in popular special events. Resnick says:

> We use the least powerful reinforcement that will work. If the child is at a stage where all he needs is the materials, then he can do it on that basis, and when he is finished we say, "That was great." If he's at the stage—and this is more typical at the beginning—where that's a long time to work without some kind of support, we arrange to have the teacher or aide essentially drop by and attend to him, using social reinforcers of any kind natural to her, while he's engaged in the task. The critical point is not to wait until the child drifts away from the task.
>
> If we aren't having great luck with social reinforcement, we'll go to a token economy. We're using that in one classroom experimentally. In most of the others we feel we will be able to manage with social reinforcement. We believe this is probably a difference in the entering skill of the teacher rather than in the entering skills of the children. The tokens are one way of getting the teacher to focus her attention more constructively.

Bushell makes this point very strongly. In comparing teachers who are using tokens with those who are not, he finds that the frequency with which a teacher attends to individual children and praises them for correct performance increases greatly when she has tokens to dispense with her praise. It would seem that the tangible quality of the token has value in underlining the occurrence of reinforcement for both the teacher and the child, at least in the early stages of a program.

Motivation: Ethical Considerations ✻

As we discussed the issues of intrinsic motivation versus external reinforcement with sponsors of different viewpoints, we began to feel that there were some rather basic philosophical and even moral issues involved—issues that were only partly verbalized, but that tapped strong emotions. The behavior-shaping approach to education is thought by many to be coercive, to imply lack of respect for the child as a human being with rights to choose what is best for his own interests, within the limitations of his knowledge. Some people even feel there are overtones of totalitarianism.

Armington, sponsor of the EDC program, expresses his belief that the use of reinforcements, or incentives, amounts to a form of coercion:

(Do you ever deliberately use incentives to get a child to work on a task?)
Just as we would be opposed to manipulating adults, we are opposed to manipulating children. It isn't necessary to design artificial and contrived ways of getting them to do what you want them to do.

Zimiles, of Bank Street, also expresses concern about what he sees as the coercive and manipulative elements of reinforcement methods:

There is a profound difference between an educational stance that is committed to the development of competence through self-awareness and autonomy, and one that teaches a child how to exact gratification from an authority by behaving according to his expectations.

Gotkin opposes assigning children to specific groups and prefers to have them enter and leave groups according to their own choice, even if this procedure is sometimes less efficient:

(What would you do about a child who didn't want to learn?)
You don't fight him, but you go about getting him in. But I wouldn't have a rigid assignment to an activity.
(Why not?)
The question is, Do the ends justify the means? And—are there other ways?
(What is the advantage of letting them come and go as they please?)
The main advantage is, it's the kind of world I believe in. If it was your own kids, you would want them to have individual freedom of choice. It is a beautiful moment when the kids are managing one of our listening centers on their own.

In contrast, Becker strongly defends the right—indeed the duty—of the educator to influence children and to set up incentive systems so that they will be influenced readily and efficiently:

People seem to be questioning the "morality" of training children, of teaching them, or influencing others. It's not unlike the attacks made against the early people in medical fields, where they found new ways of curing diseases. "It's immoral to interfere with life processes, with God's will," people used to say. They are challenging the use of the knowledge that we have to help people be better people, and here we're talking about helping people to be better parents, better friends, better teachers. I just can't see that it's immoral.

People who know about the behavior modification programs only at a distance sometimes assume that the children will be frightened and cowed when they are subjected to rapid-fire questioning, or that they will look like robots when a group is shouting out responses in unison, as the E-B program requires them to do. Judging by our experience, a visitor to an E-B classroom will be impressed by the eager excitement and enthusiasm of most of the children for what they are doing. As in every program, much depends on the skill of the individual teacher. But it seems clear that behavior-shaping programs can be run in such a way as to elicit a great deal of positive motivation and feeling in the children. Indeed, we wondered whether such feeling might be in some cases overintense: The pace was very fast and looked to the out-sider as though it might occasionally be exhausting for both the teachers and the children. There is the possibility that when the child is very intensely involved in the task, and consequences that are important to him are contingent on his performance, he will be upset if he is unable to do what is demanded of him. In a program that makes extensive use of reinforcement, it becomes doubly important that the tasks be properly paced to the in-dividual child's level of skill, so that failure will be rare.

The matter of "pace" in teaching perhaps deserves emphasis in its own right, although it is difficult to describe. The proportion of classroom time in which an individual child is being actively taught face to face by a teacher is much greater in some programs than in others. E-B philosophy is that Head Start and Follow-Through programs must be in a hurry—that they are trying to teach in a brief time what children from middle-class homes have had much more time to learn. They therefore feel that each day—each hour—the child spends in the program is precious, and if it is not spent in active teaching, something has been lost. As Engelmann says, "The name of the game is *teaching!*" Within the active-teaching portion of the day, they strive for a fast pace. The slower-paced programs tend to be the ones in which the teaching is not so structured—where teachers use the child's own spontane-ously selected activities as the occasion for teaching. We do not know whether this conjunction between pace and program philos-ophy is accidental; perhaps it is a deliberate matter of program policy among those who believe that learning must involve "dis-covery" and/or integration of new material into existing concepts, to give the child time to think between inputs of new material. At Bank Street it is thought to be important not to interrupt a child's self-chosen sequential activity—to do so would be to interfere with the development of task persistence. Decisions about pacing the teaching effort are often influenced by considerations of this kind.

Developing Autonomous Learners ✳

But to return to the various approaches to motivation: The program that emphasizes intrinsic motivation does so in part because it believes that to do so makes the child into a "self-propelled learner," who will come to be able to work effectively with minimal dependence upon the teacher. Nimnicht discusses self-propelled learning when he talks about the way the automated typewriter is designed to provide its own feedback, and how the children are allowed simply to play with it until they discover how it works:

(Would the child have lost anything if you had told him, "By the way, this typewriter doesn't work if you press two keys down together"?)
I don't know if we would have lost anything. You are hitting at the softest area of our program in terms of being able to test what we are doing. I am making an assumption—based on *some* evidence, I think—that the ages three to five are crucial ages for forming a mental set, and I am concerned about this mental set. The kind of mental set I would like to see a child possess—well, let's hypothesize the ideal person of twenty-five; this is someone who is capable of taking on unknown problems and finding solutions for them, and who has a self-confidence that he is willing to do that without a great deal of additional help. Okay, going back to ages three to five, this means it's a desirable sign—something I am trying to create—if they are willing to work these things through without having it explained to them.

The Tucson program has a similar objective. Henderson says:

We are trying to make the children into self-propelled learners. The teachers say that the Follow-Through children are more self-motivated than children in standard classrooms. In the better classrooms, the children enjoy learning.

Henderson comments that some of his own emphasis on self-motivation grew out of his earlier experience in teaching teen-age Mexican-American children. He says that they had been taught to read using a phonics method, and that the previous teaching had been successful in the sense that the children could pronounce almost any new word that you presented to them. But they were not readers—they systematically avoided reading whenever they could. Transmitting skills, then, is not enough.

Resnick also considers self-motivation as an ultimate objective, but feels that children must go through a period of fairly structured teaching before one can begin to work on producing motivational autonomy:

> We're concerned with the curriculum, and also with the shaping of motivational and attentional skills, which I call self-management skills.
> (Do you get self-management through reinforcement techniques?) We use reinforcement techniques to mediate. The goal would be what Nimnicht starts with: autotelic. I think it's theoretically possible to set up an autotelic environment that would so capture interest and also guide it in the direction of learning so that it would work. I think it's extremely difficult to do, and takes more resources than we now have available in the way of high-feedback devices— or more people. We do aim for the kind of motivation that will allow the child to work in a nonprogramed environment, because most environments will be nonprogramed, and if we want a generalized learning skill, the child has to have something that's not specific to our setting. On the other hand, we feel we must take the kids where they are, and if they're not intrinsically motivated when we get them, we're not going to be pious about it. The problem is, How do you get off the systematic reinforcement, how do you gradually fade it out, extend your schedule of reinforcement, and allow the child to work for self-generated mediated reinforcements? We have a good theory concerning this, and virtually no research. That's the main thing we want to study now: How to get children off the reinforcement without losing the behavior.

The reinforcement theorist, then, usually has the same objectives as the believer in "intrinsic" motivation: He would like to see the child become a person who learns on his own initiative, who is not dependent on frequent or artificial reinforcement from a teacher in order to learn. However, the two schools of thought differ on the means for bringing this about. The reinforcement theorist sees the process of producing independence as involving a gradual stretching out of the schedule of reinforcement: The child is first reinforced by the teacher for every correct response, then for every fifth one, and so on, until the behavior can be sustained when reinforcement is very rare. The opposing viewpoint is that one must not develop a child's dependence on the teacher's reinforcement in the first place; that she should be there to guide the child into good solution strategies, but that his reinforcement should come directly from the materials he is working with and the pleasure he will get out of success in problem solving.

To our knowledge, evaluation procedures comparing the effectiveness of the various programs have not attempted to assess how self-sustained the children's learning actually is. It would be possible to watch to see what happens when the teacher goes out of the classroom—whether the children find something to work on, or whether they sit passively or engage in horseplay. This has not yet been done in any systematic way.

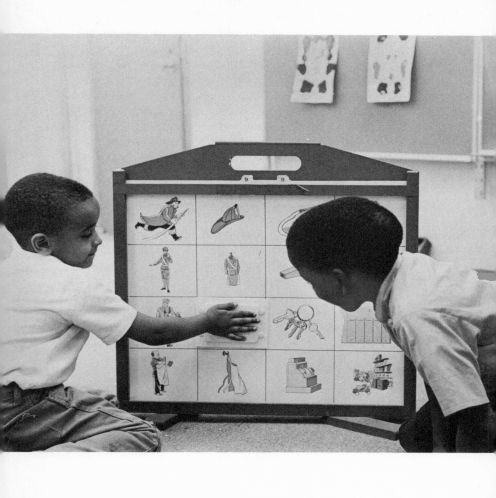

5*

The Classroom Environment
and
Its Implications for Self-Esteem

So far our comparison of the various educational philosophies involved in Follow-Through has centered on their views of what the learning process is and how children develop an interest in learning. Here we show how the implications of these theories extend to the classroom environment. Every sponsor we have interviewed has a goal of enabling all children in his program to be successful in school. Motivation, competence, self-esteem, and success are seen as profoundly interconnected. We begin this chapter by examining just how a classroom environment of competition or cooperation can be related to success and self-esteem. Then we discuss the ways in which Follow-Through programs help develop school-appropriate behavior, why behavior problems tend to vanish in Follow-Through classrooms, and how a classroom environment is created in which children can enjoy working and learning.

Cooperation, Competition, and Self-Esteem ✳

Incentives and rewards (tangible or social) are fairly widely used in Project Follow-Through as a means of drawing children into a learning situation. Some sponsors object to the use of tangible reinforcers, arguing that it is very difficult to give one child a reinforcer without producing an aversive situation for another child, at least by implication. We have here the age-old problem of competition and its effects on children's self-confidence and on their fear of failure. Nimnicht puts it this way:

> If you are concerned with helping the child to develop a positive self-image, then you will not use methods that tend not to foster that. For example, a star on one's child's forehead is a not-star for other children's foreheads. So you won't use stars as rewards because this is not fostering the self-concept that the other children have. You won't criticize the language of the home for the same reason.

Bushell protests that this same objection could be made to the use of social reinforcement:

> If a star on one child's forehead is a not-star for other children's foreheads, then it follows that praise or a compliment to one child is not-praise or not-compliment to other children. Hence, from this point of view, children should never be praised, complimented, or reinforced. How are you going to build a positive self-image without these things? Of course, any kind of potential reward *can* be used coercively, but that usually occurs in a withdrawal strategy (Mummy won't love you if you do that) rather than as praise. In classrooms that use reinforcement procedures properly, you won't see invidious distinctions, threats of loss, fines, or other abusive tactics.

In part the problem seems to be how an individual child's "success" is to be defined. When success means "better than" or "best," success for one child inevitably implies failure for another.

To avoid this quandary, a different model of success is commonly sought—one in which everyone can be a winner, and everyone can feel competent and *be* competent. In this approach the child can compete against a standard of excellence, or against his own previous performance; he may try to do better than he himself did the day before, but he need not compete against other children.

Henderson argues that excessive competitiveness in a classroom sometimes results from the fact that reinforcement is a "scarce commodity." If the teacher alone is dispensing praise or attention, it is almost inevitable that children will compete against one another for the teacher's approval. A solution is to teach children to give praise, attention, and approval to one another. Halene Weaver, of the Tucson program, describes it this way:

> One of the definite goals of the Tucson program has been to show a concern for the other human beings in the class. A child who meets a visitor in our classroom will very likely say, "Come and see what so-and-so has done," rather than, "Come and see what I've done." This concern is not only for other individuals, but for the group as a whole or for a small group. "Come and see what my committee has done. Come see what Raoul's committee has done." This kind of thing goes on all the time in our classroom, and there is a definite reinforcement for this kind of behavior.

In programs that deliberately attempt to foster cooperation and group identification, the classroom frequently gives the impression of being a small community. It is the children's workroom and they assume responsibility for it. In the EDC program this is called an "open classroom." Typically, there is a variety of activities going on simultaneously, and the children choose for themselves what to work on and whether to work with others or alone. There is great flexibility in terms of time schedules, activities, and groupings of children. What goes on and the way the classroom is arranged and decorated reflect the interests of the children. The teacher provisions the environment, to be sure, but her role is to support and guide rather than to dictate.

Teachers in these programs encourage children to pursue their own interests. Working with other children—learning together, teaching, and learning from one another—is seen as in no way antithetical to individual achievement, as this comment from Halene Weaver illustrates:

> Although we do have a goal of having the children show concern for other human beings and other children's work, it's not *instead* of their own, because we do build self-concept and we do have children who are very proud of the "I can-ness" within them. We recognize competence in whatever form it occurs in others or in ourselves. Children in our classrooms are very wise in psyching out who can do a thing best, and they know where to go for help.

Zimiles, of Bank Street, although generally advocating the fostering of cooperative behavior, cautions against too much emphasis on it too soon:

> We found that many of the children did not have enough satisfaction from their products and didn't know what they wanted. It seemed necessary at the beginning to direct a lot of attention to encouraging children to protect what they had chosen or made, and [to] enjoy it. I would worry about a program that rushes right into supporting, sharing, and altruism. First you've got to cultivate a sense of self before you can move to these other-directed levels.

Cooperation and competition need not, of course, be polar opposites. In some educational settings the two approaches are combined by having groups or teams of children compete against one another. The child then learns cooperation within his own group, while maintaining an often fierce competitive spirit toward other groups. Bronfenbrenner† reports that this approach is extensively employed in Soviet schools, where, for example, the first row of the classroom may compete against the second row. We did not find this particular device being employed in Follow-Through programs. Perhaps the nearest thing to it occurs in classrooms being run according to the behavior modification approach, where the competition is usually with the teacher, not with other

† Urie Bronfenbrenner, *Two Worlds of Childhood* (New York: Russell Sage Foundation, 1970).

children. The teacher, of course, only pretends to compete, and more often than not she concedes: "You beat me. You're too smart for me." The children are delighted and work hard for these victories.

There is considerable ambivalence in Follow-Through programs over competition and its proper role in the classroom. David Seeley, of the Public Education Association, comments:

> I think our society is going to go through some very fundamental changes in this regard. Certainly it's coming at us in the "Community Control" districts in New York. I detect a real drive for cutting down the aggressive-competitive drive, which John Whiting says is very typical of our Yankee culture, and a much greater drive toward finding a way in which people help each other learn, and all succeed. I think we're going to have to adjust in some way to the whole original Calvinistic business, and [to] develop some kind of combination of competition and cooperation that we haven't yet developed.

Kenneth Haskins, the former principal of the Morgan Community School in Washington, D.C., had Follow-Through activities in some of his classrooms. He expresses a distinctively black point of view about competition:

> You really don't understand. When we say we want the things that you have, that doesn't mean we want to be the way that you are. Just because somebody wants a comfortable house, that doesn't mean that he has to be a very competitive person with all kinds of degrees, who still can't stop competing with people because whoever programed him will never make him satisfied. If I had a choice for my kid and knew it, there are some problems that well-educated white people have that I would never want my kid to have, even if he functioned at a lower level according to someone's definition of what's intellectually acceptable.

Some argue that, whatever one's personal values in the matter, it is irresponsible to instill primarily cooperative values in children when these are not shared or rewarded by the rest of the culture. To ignore the present realities may mean that one increases the chances of the child's experiencing failure when he leaves the relatively protected environment of a Follow-Through classroom. Others insist that there is no reason to lead children into capitulating in advance to values that ought to be changed.

These pervasive value issues aside, it is generally agreed that the way teachers handle competition and cooperation in a classroom has a bearing on how the child comes to see himself— whether he thinks of himself as a success or a failure.

The development of self-esteem—of a positive self-concept —is seen by a number of people as central to the process of developing a child's motivation to learn on his own. A child who does not see himself as a person deserving of the respect of others will be apathetic and passive; furthermore, he will be fatalistic— will feel that he has little control over his own fate—and these states of mind are inimical to learning. Nimnicht stresses the family origins of the self-concept:

> If his parents have not done well in schools, they have low levels of aspiration for him and this is conveyed to him. If the father is not in the home, and the mother is demeaning about men, and you happen to be a boy, you fall into this pattern. If you are in a large family, you don't get much attention, and you soon discover that you are really a nuisance—at least you feel that way, whether it is true or not. If your parents are psychologically defeated—have given up, accepted their lot, and feel that they don't have any effect upon their own lives—this impression is also conveyed to the child. All of these things tend to affect the way the child sees himself and his intellectual development.

Repeatedly, teachers and sponsors commented on how traditional schools have compounded this sense of defeat among many minority-group children. Gotkin, in addition to developing instructional games, has attempted to help the children feel a sense of self-worth by bringing some of the music of their own culture into the classrooms. He has encountered a good deal of resistance to this innovation:

Some of the resistance to using this kind of music is that it's not dignified enough. But when they say that, they're saying things about the kid's parents. It makes it harder for the kid to feel at home in the school.

(How about your strategy of teaching with games?)

Kids and adults feel more at home playing games, and that makes the instructional job easier. It also makes the kid feel more accepting of his own background. I don't see why because you're after direct instruction that you can't do it in a way that says some other very important things that are closely related to what the whole black revolution is about. Their heritage, their home lives have been basically rejected by the institutions that are to socialize them. If the children move rhythmically in school, the whole damn school has been saying to them, "Sit up. Don't move." And they've been brought up in a way that involves a lot of movement. You're fighting the kids all the way if you don't work with that instead of against it.

In some programs lessons are designed about the culture and history of a minority group, with the intent of enhancing the children's pride in their ethnic identity. The hope is that if the children's self-esteem can be improved in this way, they will be more interested in tackling the subject matter of the school curriculum.

Haskins stresses how the atmosphere of a traditional school is such as to demean and frighten the child:

When I first came to the school, I couldn't reach my hand out and touch a child on the shoulder without him pulling away. The whole pattern of relationships was like an immate-prison-guard kind of thing. My major focus at the beginning was to try to break that down. I tried to make the climate one in which the children could feel that this school was theirs. We introduced a good number of people from the community to work in the school. This helped some, but many times they believed in handling kids in a pretty rough way; but somehow, they were able to do it without looking down their noses at the kid in the same way a middle-class person does.

We've tried to make the school a human place. We've tried

to address it to the children in the way that children are, assuming that children do not have to be put into a kind of straitjacket in order to learn. Things like running in the hall are nothing to concern yourself about in that sense.

Haskins argues that the children must feel that their normal ways of speaking, dressing, and moving are accepted in the schools; and he believes that the racial and social-class origins of the adults working in the school have an important bearing on whether this acceptance can be genuine.

Teachers and directors in all the programs agree that in-school experiences should be such as to foster a sense of self-worth among the children being taught. There is disagreement, however, as to whether a program needs to take direct measures to achieve this end. On the whole, the Skinnerians have tended to take the view that low self-esteem is a consequence, rather than a cause, of poor performance. They say that once the child acquires some dependable skills, he will begin to feel like a competent person and will be more willing to tackle new tasks. Becker, of the E-B program, comments:

> Certainly, building competence is an essential basis for self-esteem, but the way you build competence is also important, and we do this through the use of positive reinforcement. If you tell kids they're good and they're doing a good job and they're doing it the right way, they start saying, "I'm good. I do it the right way. I'm a good guy." And that's what self-esteem is about. "I'm smart. You can't trick me." This is what we're talking about, and you build it by the way you talk to kids. You can do it inadvertently, or you can do it more directly.

From this point of view, a program that concentrates most of its efforts directly on the development of academic skills through reinforcement will not be neglecting the children's self-esteem.

Task Orientation, Attention, and
School-Appropriate Behavior *

In all programs it is recognized that certain school-appropriate behavior—what used to be called "deportment"—is necessary if the child is to be susceptible to teaching. Resnick stresses the importance of the children's learning to maintain task orientation before specific teaching can begin:

> We ask what it is we want the children to do, and we describe the behaviors as carefully as we can. At the beginning these things are some of the simple self-managing things: going to a shelf, taking materials, playing with them in nondestructive ways—this is at the beginning when they haven't yet been taught specific things to do with the materials. We describe these behaviors and concentrate on those management skills plus building attention span in those children who are lacking it, without very much concern for what they're doing—just engagement with the materials over more and more extended periods is what we try to get in the beginning.

Bushell describes his concept of the desired behavior as follows:

> Several categories of "academic skill" may be identified, but one frequently overlooked is that constellation of behaviors which make up the social role of the student. Children who say "Good morning" to their teachers, who raise their hands when appropriate, who can distinguish between the time to talk and the time to be silent, who can stay with an assigned task, and who respond appropriately to the praise and compliments of the teacher, possess skills which are advantageous to the control of their school environment. Skill in this category, as well as with other academic facts, must be developed if a child is to compete successfully in the school system.

Bushell is defining the kind of behavior that is necessary for a child to function effectively in a traditional classroom. Programs that place less emphasis on routine and structure also stress the need for maintaining a "working atmosphere" in the classroom, although what this means is very different from one program to another. A Bank Street working paper states:

> For the five-, six-, and seven-year-old, the effective classroom is an organized, efficient workroom, where there is opportunity for motor and sensory experiences, for active investigation of what things are and how they work. Working in this room, with its understandable rules and well-defined physical structure, the children are able to control and organize themselves and to develop skills for mastery in their environment. As the children go about their work, they move and talk freely.

In such a classroom, a child would probably not be required to raise his hand if he wanted the teacher's attention. Nevertheless, despite the informality of the classroom, there are certain rationally based "rules" about permissible classroom behavior. Even in the "ultrafree" environment of a Summerhill classroom, where a child need not remain in the classroom or stay with an assigned task if he wishes to leave it, there is a limit to the child's individual freedom. He cannot behave continuously in such a way as to interfere with the freely chosen learning activities of other children.

It has been widely observed that behavior problems tend to diminish radically, or even disappear, in Follow-Through classrooms as the program progresses. This is true in programs that differ widely in their pedagogical methods. Here are some of the comments that were made to us on this subject:

> WEIKART: When the teachers aren't teaching, when they feel there's no respect for their work, they begin to see all kinds of faults in the kids, and you find that they are referring large numbers of kids out for outside help of all sorts—remedial reading, psychotherapy, and so on. We find that we don't have to refer kids for outside help from our Follow-Through classrooms. When the school refers a child out for "help," it is really trying to remove an irritant, not save the kid. The saving of kids has got to occur right in the regular classroom.

R E S N I C K : We help the teachers to ignore infractions unless they become violent or truly disruptive, in which case they're handled by time out. I suppose we'd have to go to more serious punishment if we had more serious infractions, but frankly we haven't had a misbehavior in more than three and a half months. If you're talking to Follow-Through people, you've probably not been hearing of behavior problems, because all of them, whether they're working on reinforcement theory or not, are providing the kids a positive experience that essentially preempts it.

H E N D E R S O N : We have very few discipline problems. In an eastern city, some people came to observe our demonstration classes, and they were amazed at the absence of discipline problems. It's just the frequent opportunities for success that do a lot to cut down on this kind of problem.

Some programs attempt to train specifically for attentiveness. We observed a teacher in an E-B program working with a group of five children on conjunction. On several occasions she noticed that one child was slumping in his chair and letting his gaze wander around the room. On each such occasion she praised another child in the group for sitting up and paying attention ("See, Johnny knows how to sit up nicely"), and each time the inattentive child reoriented himself to the task. When a competitive game was being played in which the teacher and the children were trying to see who could call out the correct name for a portion of a picture the fastest, the teacher pointed to the ceiling and said, "See that bird up there?" and then quickly pointed to the picture while one or two of the children were looking away. Then she praised the children who had not been distracted ("Darn it, Johnny, I couldn't fool you and you beat me"). Thus there was specific reinforcement for resisting distraction.

In several programs it is considered coercive to guide children too directly into task-oriented behavior. Gordon found that some of his aides and visiting mothers would say to a child, "You sit here with me" when they wanted the child to work on something, and his program called for training the aides and mothers to be less directive. Likewise, it is part of the philosophy of the Nimnicht program that classroom materials and activities should be interest-

ing enough to attract the children; it should never be necessary to
say, "Be quiet," or "Pay attention," and if this is heard frequently
in a classroom, something is wrong with the level of the materials
being used. Hughes, of Tucson, makes a similar point:

> Teachers have to learn to be responsive to children, the kind of re-
> sponse that supports the child, that invites him to think, to work.
> Very few teachers do this intuitively. The teachers spend much of
> their time in discipline, insisting that their children listen, as it were.
> We try to eliminate these kinds of concepts entirely, because you
> invite the child not to think or pay attention. You handle the ma-
> terials so that the materials make the demand; what's going on is so
> interesting that he has to pay attention. Then we reward him for his
> interest in the materials, but we don't reward him for turning
> toward us.

In the E-B program, by contrast, when a teacher sees a child
wandering unoccupied around the room, she is allowed or even
encouraged to say, "Come on over here, I want to teach you something." As we noted above, in this program the view is that there
is not time to wait for the child's interest to develop spontaneously,
and that this interest can be aroused by exposing him to the task,
if the teaching is skillful.

Bushell argues that "attention span" is a false concept. One
only needs to remember, he says, how long the average five- or six-
year-old child can remain absorbed in a television program to
realize that the traditional view about attention span (that young
children can concentrate on an enterprise for only a few minutes at
a time) is false. Extended task orientation and persistence at
school-related tasks are aspects of behavior that can be taught.
And disruptive behavior can also be dealt with directly:

> Suppose a child is creating a problem by talking to his neighbors
> during a lesson. Rather than having to nag, scold, or threaten pun-
> ishment for such behavior, the teacher may simply offer the child
> the opportunity to engage in the undesirable behavior for a set
> period of time by "buying" a license for it with tokens. If the cost
> of the license is rather high, the child will generally elect to ter-

minate the behavior rather than use up most of his tokens to buy the license. This is not to suggest that misbehavior is treated as a privilege. It merely illustrates one of several procedures which are effective in dealing with children in ways which avoid punishment and abuse.

More commonly, in programs with a behavior modification orientation, the teachers are urged to ignore undesirable behavior and give their attention to a child only when he is engaged in constructive, task-oriented behavior. The principle underlying this practice is, of course, that the teacher's attention is reinforcing, and if she goes to the child when he is behaving badly (even if the attention takes the form of scolding or discipline), she is strengthening the very behavior she wishes to eliminate. In practice it is not possible to ignore a child's actions if he is injuring other children or seriously disrupting their work. The behavior modification programs usually handle this kind of situation by "time out"—temporarily removing the child from the group. At Bank Street, and in the EDC program, the disruptive behavior is seen as a signal that the child needs attention and help, and teachers attempt to give it. They believe that a child needs to feel that he is basically accepted whatever he may do. But the acceptance is accompanied by efforts to reorient the child. An exchange between Zimiles, Gotkin, and Resnick illustrates some differences of opinion on this subject:

(Do you have confidence that accepting that behavior ultimately leads to its modification?)

Z I M I L E S : No. Mere acceptance is not enough, but it is a first step. Some kind of strategy with regard to each individual child is needed. Certainly, a basic premise is that the children have to feel that this is an environment where they are accepted.

R E S N I C K : The most effective technique for getting rid of these unacceptable behaviors is to ignore them. Would you consider that to be accepting it or not? Just walk around the child until he stops. And then go to him right away.

Z I M I L E S : If we thought that a child was being inordinately provocative and demanding attention, we would try to give it to him, but in a particular way. We would try to understand what his behavior means. We would observe him carefully in the classroom. He is helped to express his feelings verbally or through play. The teacher will try to find a way of responding to his work or structuring the social situation so that the child is more capable of coping with it. The role of the adult is always to make explicit the reality and demands of the situation in which the child is having difficulty, and to arrange his classroom life so that he can cope with it successfully.

GOTKIN : Practical problem: A kid brushes by another kid, and the kid who's brushed by belts him. I remember a little girl saying, "My Mamma told me to." This has been taught to kids, that you protect yourself. The business of ignoring does not help when one kid is belting another, because the other kid hits back.

RESNICK: Well, but if we *do* ignore it, we can just show the behavior going away!

In all the behavior modification programs, there is an explicit policy of avoiding punishing the children for "bad" behavior. Many people have told us, however, that the policy is often difficult to implement because the teachers and teachers' aides have been so accustomed to using punishment before coming into Follow-Through classrooms. In some programs that allow "time out" as a *last* resort for treatment of behavior that is too disruptive to be tolerated, some teachers tend to use the time-out device punitively and as a *first* resort. However, the number of occasions on which teachers judge that any punishment is necessary declines as the children develop positive interest in the curriculum. When interest in the curriculum materials is *not* high, children begin to "float" in an unorganized way around the classroom, looking for something to do, and many teachers take this as a danger sign that explosive interpersonal behavior may develop among the children.

A number of people recognize variations in what might be called "classroom mood"—that there are some days when a whole classroom of children are "high," and other days when they settle down easily into a good working mood. It was surprising to us how infrequently the sponsors refer to psychoanalytically based "dynamic" concepts in describing these emotional states of children, or in discussing how such states should be handled. Gotkin, however, says:

> Sometimes you shift the activity—take them for a walk—or use gross muscle activity. Try to convert the energy into something.

And Nimnicht mentions having the children sing as loud as they can as one of several techniques for handling groups of children who seem unduly excited. There is some psychodynamic emphasis in the EDC program as well. Armington says:

> A child who comes into this environment and has difficulties very often will outlive them, and much more quickly than he would in a tight situation where the first thing they do is to call in a psychologist. In a sense this kind of an environment is therapeutic because it provides far more opportunity than a conventional school environment for a child to become involved in things that matter to him. If a child has aggressions that he wants to let out, there is clay he can pound, wood he can saw, and nails that he can hammer. It is fair to go out into the corridor or playground and engage in dramatic play, where he can give vent to his inner feelings. This is all legitimate school activity.

Other program sponsors strongly disagree with the proposition that encouraging a child to pound clay in any way "gets aggression out of his system," or makes him less likely to hit another child. In any case, the primary point, agreed upon by people of widely differing viewpoints, is that inattentiveness and disruptive behavior are usually consequences, not causes, of poor learning.

Teachers and school administrators can clearly see that noisy, disruptive, aggressive behavior interferes with the teaching objectives of a school. Many educators insist that the opposite sort of behavior—frightened passivity or withdrawal—is just as inimical to learning, although its effects are not so apparent to the casual observer. Many minority-group children are afraid of their teachers, of the other children, or of the school itself. Zimiles, from his work at Bank Street, observes:

It's been our experience that the kids feel they live in a dangerous world. When they play, many of their themes revolve around death and danger. The first important step is to get them to perceive the school as a comprehensible and reliable environment, and that can take a long time and much of our initial work is devoted to it. Because of that, we have found that we have to introduce more structure. We're not as fluid or flexible as we are when we work with middle-class children. The need to create order and maintain it and establish predictability requires that we adhere to a more consistent and stereotyped day, from day to day.

Haskins, as noted earlier, is also much concerned with the fearfulness that he finds in the children in a ghetto school. He feels, however, that a school should respond to this by *decreasing* the amount of "structure" in the school routine—at least, he advocates a drastic reduction in the number and severity of rules governing the child's behavior:

The first thing I did [when I became principal]—and this would go for any school—is that I looked at all the rules and regulations, and those that didn't make any sense we eliminated. Those that were ridiculous we examined. So that if a kid is late, you don't send him down to the office to get a pass, because that only makes him later. If you are really interested in the kid being in school, you'll be glad to see him no matter when he comes. There are junior high schools where it's easier for a kid to miss a whole day than to come ten minutes late. And chewing gum is not a crime.

(What about lining up?)

We don't do that. They come in any of the doors that are open, and they can go up or down all the stairways. If you want to teach a child to say "Excuse me" when he interrupts two adults, you say "Excuse me" when you interrupt two children, and they will learn. If you cut down on all the rules, you very quickly find that the instances of negative contact between adults and children diminish, and you have instead a social relationship that's very different, and children begin to use the adult for learning much more easily.

Kids are free to move around the building, so there are things people might call therapeutic that are natural. I have fourth-grade kids who maybe once or twice a week go down to the kindergarten, and they may play with the materials—or they might say they're helping kindergarten children. I don't know whether this is a time when they want relief from the pressure of their own room, or want to handle things they're very confident of handling, or what, but they're free to do it. The only rule I have is that if they go someplace, they don't annoy the people there. I think there are some who hang out in a room because the teacher is pretty. I really don't look into all the reasons because I don't emphasize pathology. If there's room to move around, and if the kid doesn't bother anybody, then I don't need to know whether he does what he does because there's no father in the home or because his mother just had a baby.

In short, whereas Zimiles says that a school environment must be *predictable* in order to make a child feel secure, Haskins stresses that it must not be restrictive or coercive.

6 *

Parent Participation

Up till now, we have been discussing psychological theories—or perhaps more accurately, educational philosophies—as they affect the way a teacher deals with a child in the classroom. In a number of programs it is felt that a child cannot learn effectively in the classroom unless he is simultaneously receiving some support for his learning at home. Several programs bring mothers into the classroom as teachers' aides. Others carry the programs into the children's homes, with systematic efforts to teach the mothers to teach the children. Gordon's project has placed special emphasis on this kind of work. In this book it is not possible to do complete justice to the parent-involvement aspects of the Follow-Through programs. Let us simply summarize some of the issues that are involved.

Educating Parents *

First of all, the programs that emphasize parent participation or parent training usually assume that at least part of the intellectual deficit of the "deprived" child stems from the nature of the inter-action patterns that exist in the home. We quote Gordon:

A program has to start early and last long and include the home environment as well as the child. We have only been attempting to manipulate *some* of the affective and cognitive variables in the mother. We have not reached the father, nor have we conceptually figured out how to go about doing that. Nor have we dealt with the basic life-support system—food, shelter, density, and so forth. What some of our mothers need is not someone to be concerned about their self-esteem, they need some food and a better place to live in. Our problem very often is sheer apathy. A little aggression would be welcome. If the mother's apathy stems from malnourishment, then there's a real question about whether she's going to get much out of spending an hour or so a week with our parent educator, learning something to do with her child.

Apart from the direct effects of poverty on the child's "life-support system," there is fairly general agreement that what might be called the Hess and Shipman† syndrome characterizes the mother-child interaction found in the homes of many Follow-Through children. This syndrome is variously described. It usually involves maternal inattention and unresponsiveness to the child. The language mothers use to the children is impoverished, even if the mothers are capable of more sophisticated constructions in talking to others. The mothers tend to have little self-confidence and to feel that they have little control over their own fate. Life in the home is disorganized; things do not occur predictably. In terms of their cognitive functioning, Gordon finds that many of the parents are as "pre-operational" as the children. They are literal and situation-bound in what they do. For example, a home visitor was trying to show a mother how to stimulate an infant by having him follow an object moving across his field of vision. The visitor illustrated this by moving his car keys in front of the baby. The mother felt that she could not carry out this procedure with the baby by herself because she did not have any car keys; it did not occur to her to use another object.

Of course, the Hess and Shipman syndrome occurs in a cer-

† R. D. Hess and Virginia Shipman, "Early Experience and the Socialization of Cognitive Modes in Children," *Child Development*, Vol. 36 (1965), pp. 869–86.

tain proportion of white middle-class homes too; it is not confined to the culture of poverty. But the conditions of life that accompany poverty and minority-group status probably increase the frequency of its occurrence among the families served by Follow-Through.

Program sponsors differ over how common they believe these kinds of maternal characteristics are. They also differ over whether it is essential for a Follow-Through program to try to deal with them directly, no matter how common they may be. Some programs regularly send teachers, or "parent educators," into the homes of the enrolled children to show the mother some of the tasks and materials being used in the classrooms, to show her how to present these and similar tasks to the child, and to show her how to tell whether the child is interested and has understood what was presented to him. People working with the mothers comment that after a few sessions of this kind, the mother begins to be much more aware of her child's reactions, and begins to take pride in small cognitive accomplishments that previously would not have meant anything to her.

Richard Dunham, who is developing an educational program in a community in the South (not part of Follow-Through), says:

We have had some good results from involving the child and the mother in a half-day-every-day program for almost two years. It tends to confirm the idea that it is not only cognitive factors that have to be influenced, but things like disciplinary style and the non-cognitive parts of what has been called "teaching style." While our mothers came in characteristically resorting to aversive controls, after about six months in the program, less than 10 percent of their disciplinary actions toward children were punitive. The rest were rewarding and encouraging. With this change in disciplinary pattern there sprung up among the mothers a trust of each other. About that same time, the fathers began to wonder whether they should disapprove of this change in child-rearing policies, so we had to work through with them what their attitudes would be. In the long run, the families have strong educational aspirations for themselves as well as [for] their children, and we are now placing the mothers as teaching aides. We are led toward an increasing emphasis on the family. It may be time to call for long-term, whole family, experimental intervention.

The programs that include parent education efforts of this kind seem to act on the following assumption: If the cognitive deficits of "disadvantaged" children stem, at least in some cases, from deficiencies in the nature of their interaction with their parents, then the best way to repair these deficits is to improve that interaction. This assumption is only beginning to be put to empirical tests. Its validity would seem to rest on comparing the remedial efficiency of parent-oriented efforts with the effectiveness of a similar expenditure of effort in direct work with the child.

Other programs are less concerned with supplying "compensatory" education for either parent or child and see themselves rather as enriching or extending the existing skills and culture of the population with whom they are working. In some cases parent education also includes demonstrating to the parents the benefits of a system of education that is quite unlike anything they had anticipated. Armington, of the EDC program, presents this position:

> I see no reason to question the view that these children are disadvantaged in terms of conventional expectations of achievement. They very often lack the linguistic skills that are necessary for school activities. But rather than try to correct these and get the children ready to perform the conventional tasks, we want to meet the children where they are, to look at the talents, the powers, that they already possess, which are really quite enormous, and to build on those and to let the life of the children unfold in ways that are natural in that particular social and cultural setting, not to constrain the child to some preconceived context.

> (You said before that the program would be part of the culture the children have, and I was wondering about what conflicts you might have with the parents who are sometimes characterized as "authoritarian." How do they feel about the program and how do you make the program have continuity with the rest of the children's lives?)

> The continuity is built-in, if you accept the culture from which he comes and extend from that base. What parents often expect is that the school is going to prepare the child to meet middle-class standards. They want the child to begin to learn to read in September of the first-grade year, and they expect him to be able to read by the end of the year. What parents lack, and indeed what many teachers lack, is a visible alternative to the way they themselves were educated. Our experience this year has been that when

parents come into a classroom where learning is proceeding very differently, they do respond in a positive way to it.

And Charles Ascheim adds:

In a ghetto there seems, quite understandably, only one way "you get farther than I got." You do what you're told, learn everything you can, pass all the tests, and make more money as a result. Those parents are likely to bring pressure of that sort: "When are you going to teach him to read?" But I don't think it's because they're authoritarian in their ideas about children; it's because they're very anxious. You try to give them a sense of a different model of success, a different way you could say your kid has gone far.

Parent views about what the schools should be doing with their children are widely divergent and sometimes rather intensely conflicting. For example, in Indian or Spanish-American communities some parent groups have brought pressure on the Follow-Through programs to use Spanish or the Indian languages in the schools. They believe that this will help the child to feel that his own culture is respected, and that it will also permit building bridges between what the child already knows—his existing linguistic skills—and the material he is asked to learn in school. When other Follow-Through programs have attempted to use the children's native languages for instruction, however, they have sometimes encountered opposition from parents who argue that the function of the schools is to prepare the child to "make it" in the larger American scene, and that to continue a child's reliance on a non-English language is simply to drive him deeper into minority-group status. To a lesser degree these same conflicts occur about other aspects of minority-group culture such as music, myths, dress, and food.

Bushell describes other sources of parent opposition to the use of a non-English language:

We have Hopi in all the classrooms in our Hopi project, but the way it was accomplished varies considerably, whether it was done carefully through the tribal council or through asking parents to come in and use it. The rationale we used was that many of the children come with limited command of English but with skill in

Hopi, and [we] have to use it to have something to teach with. Our rule is, "Say first in Hopi and repeat it in English." We've met with two kinds of resistance to the use of the Hopi language. One is among the very traditional group that doesn't want the white man's school messing around with their language. The other is with the parents who have grown up in Bureau of Indian Affairs schools, where they were hit for speaking Hopi, so they just don't want Hopi in the classrooms.

It has been Bushell's experience that parental opposition of this kind soon changes if parents have an opportunity to visit the school and see how helpful using the child's first language is in enabling him to handle the initial impact of the school curriculum.

Parent Power ✳

"Parent involvement" in Follow-Through programs has two very different meanings. In some programs, as we have seen above, it means "parent education" and may involve bringing parents into the classroom (sometimes to be trained as teacher's aides) to augment their own child-training skills and to increase their understanding of the experiences their children are undergoing at school. In other programs "parent involvement" means parent participation in the control of the programs—in the hiring of teachers and the setting of goals for the curriculum. Parent participation has been a goal of Project Follow-Through since the beginning. The original legal and administrative specifications for the program stated that in each community where there were Follow-Through classes, there would have to be a Parent Advisory Council. The membership, drawn from the community, was to share in the responsibility for deciding what kind of Follow-Through program the school would have, and was to exercise continuing advisory and review functions throughout the life of the program, to make sure that the chosen program actually met the needs of the local community.

Some programs have gone beyond the Follow-Through Guidelines and have made it a central objective to extend and strengthen the control of community representatives over the schools. Programs that deliberately try to foster parent participation in this sense are concerned with the implications of the fact that the children served by Follow-Through programs are largely from minority groups. The assumption is that when these children go to schools dominated by "white power," their school experiences will almost certainly be demeaning in countless ways. Haskins comments:

> What happens when the people who are dealing in early education for black children can stand black children but they can't stand black adults? If this is their problem, they will not be educating people to be adults; they'll be educating people to be children, and that's been a problem in this society for black people all along.

The advocates of community control argue that minority-group children can only be protected from this "education for continued subjugation" by attending schools where members of their own ethnic or racial group are in control—where the people in charge will respect them and will serve as models illustrating the fact that people of their own group can "make it" through the avenue of education. Becker, of the E-B program, describes what "parent power" means in Follow-Through:

> In the Follow-Through Guidelines, rules are provided which at least encourage the "Establishment" to talk with parents and their representatives about what the schools are doing with their kids. I've seen these Guidelines operate effectively as an instrument for institutional change. They speak directly to the issue of getting the control of schools into the hands of the consumer.
>
> In addition to the Guidelines, I believe within our program I've seen another potent force for change operating. I believe we have going within our program effective procedures for teaching children. We have also shown that parents can come into the classroom and teach children. We have a vehicle for getting parents behind us and into the school. We are developing a parent power which can be a force for institutional change. Under these conditions, the community and the school have to cooperatively interact, or quit the Follow-Through program.

The implications of the power relationship between school systems and the larger community are discussed in Chapters 7 and 8.

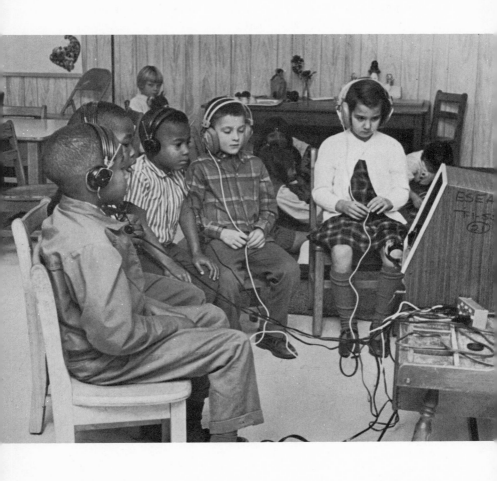

7 *

Working with Teachers
and
School Systems

So far we have devoted most of our attention to curriculum. That is, we have been discussing how programs differ in the teaching techniques they employ with children (and in some cases, mothers), and we have examined the rationale underlying the differences in pedagogical practice. Empirically, it is still an open question as to how much these variations contribute to the outcome of compensatory education programs. Weikart has compared three fairly different curricula (which do not differ in the amount of parent involvement, however). He has shown that fairly widely varying curricula can be almost equally effective if certain operational criteria are met. Let us now set aside the issues of pedagogical technique and focus on these criteria. It is the program-operational characteristics that determine whether whatever teaching techniques one wishes to employ are actually used with sufficient fidelity and frequency to give a program a chance of success.

Teaching Teachers ✳

Every Follow-Through program incorporates a chain of command. In most programs, program sponsors train trainers, who go to widely scattered school districts to work with teachers. These teachers may in their turn train teachers' aides. The teachers and the aides then teach the children and in some instances, as we have seen, the children's mothers as well. Clearly, as instructions and suggestions are transmitted through this chain, there are numerous opportunities for distortions or omissions to occur. Furthermore, there is no guarantee that the sense of dedication and purpose found among the sponsors will be found at the operational level. It can be attenuated almost to the vanishing point under adverse conditions.

Program sponsors have been giving more and more attention to the transmission process. They have come to feel that they know a good deal about how to teach an individual child, if they have him in front of them for a reasonable period of time. But knowing effective teaching techniques will do little good unless they are being delivered to many children by many teachers day after day. How to impart the necessary skills to teachers and maintain their interest and skills over extended periods of time becomes the central problem. Bushell puts the matter in this way:

Statements about Follow-Through will probably continue to stress that it seeks to change children. It should be clear, however, that our immediate objectives are to make major—even radical—changes in the teachers' behavior. We have found that there are formidable barriers to this type of change, and I think we have encountered each and every one of them. One could be called "historical events." First, many of our teachers (and principals) were *assigned* to Follow-Through without prior knowledge of its requirements, and usually lacking our conviction that departures from their familiar practices were needed. Second, there is the history which all teachers have had with innovators. As you know, criticizing education is a favorite indoor sport for nearly everyone. Early in their careers, eager teachers listen closely to the innovator's "theory" and return to the classroom to try it out. For various reasons the new theory always seems to require a little more work, but it doesn't seem to improve the performance of the children. After three or four such experiences the teacher stops listening to the "innovator." Or worse yet, she learns to look him in the eye and say, "Yes, I understand; that's very interesting." She then returns to the classroom to do her own thing.

The third set of historically established barriers to change are those institutional customs which I have come to call "excuses not to teach." My list includes IQ scores, which reassure the teacher that the inadequate progress of some students is not her fault. Grading is another well-developed device which, thanks to the normal curve, permits a teacher to say, "I taught it all right, he just didn't learn it very well." Ability grouping and the "readiness philosophy" are also on my list for similar reasons. Of special concern to Follow-Through, however, is the latest social science contribution to the list, the label "culturally deprived." Almost magically what was intended to indicate the need for more sensitive and effective education has been transformed into an excuse for educational inadequacy. As one teacher explained to me: "Ours are deprived children. You can't expect as much from them."

Halene Weaver, who has been involved in teacher training in schools in the Southwest, makes a similar point:

In implementing any program, there is a great difficulty in raising teacher expectations of what the children can do. We meet it across the board. No matter how supportive the administration, we meet the teacher resistance of, "Well, we can see the worthwhile aspects of your program, we know teachers can do it this way, but is it worth it? Because we don't think these children are ever going to learn."

If the teacher's performance is the key element in successfully introducing an experimental program, does a program director attempt to locate teachers somewhere in the school system who possess the attitudes and skills that fit the program (and perhaps even bring in new teachers from outside), or does he attempt to change the teachers who are already there? Becker strongly advocates the latter approach:

I have heard people talking about selecting teachers who were "effective"—who were nice to kids and so on. Again, the thing is, train them to be better teachers. The minute you start selecting, you're doing the same stupid thing that people do to children who don't perform well in school—you're saying, "You're no good, get out of here," instead of, "Let me show you how to do it right." We've worked with teachers whom many of you, with any selection process, would probably get rid of. We've made them into nice teachers by showing them how to say nice things to kids, how to smile, how to play. I think people can be taught to be different.

Haskins, in contrast, emphasizes teacher selection. He believes parents should be involved in interviewing new teachers before they are assigned to the school. This is part of the development of "community power" (which is discussed further in Chapter 8) and is intended to help make the teachers feel responsible to the community rather than just to a school bureaucracy.

In practice, most program directors must work with and through the existing teaching staff to a large extent. In view of the kinds of problems outlined by Bushell above, it is no surprise that systematic monitoring of the teaching process has been found to be an essential element of every successful intervention program. The monitoring can take the form of continuous and detailed testing of the children, to determine whether they have learned what was presumably being taught, or it can be some sort of systematic observation of the teacher's behavior, or both. It is by no means easy for the teachers to accept this monitoring. It has not usually been part of standard school procedures at any level. Teachers from kindergarten through college have been monarchs in their own classrooms. The problem in applied social psychology is how to introduce close supervision where none has existed before—how to get the teachers to accept the necessity of it and to feel that it is not demeaning or excessively onerous. In a number of programs it has been found helpful to work with teachers in groups, viewing videotapes of each other's teaching performance, and all joining in the critique of one another's teaching techniques. Weikart notes:

The operational issue is, What's the power of the [Follow-Through] staff? We demand planning and provide supervision. Our training-people keep the teachers focused on the curriculum principles that are involved. It's a team: The teachers work together in groups of two. I know that team teaching usually fails, but it works if the team has a supervisor who focuses their discussions on core problems, such as, "How best do we teach quantitative concepts?" Don't confuse this with the permissive situation in which the teacher has the right to do whatever she wants. That's not what I mean. But she does have the right to design her own program for her own class.

Basically, the problem is one of maintaining supervision while obtaining participation and understanding from teachers, rather than uninvolved, mechanical compliance. Many who have day-to-day contact with training-teachers (and teacher-trainers) consider it crucially important whether the program director conceives of the transmission of information about curriculum as a one-way or a two-way thing. Teachers use many phrases to describe their reactions when they are told exactly what to do, and when they work under close supervision from a trainer who observes and corrects them without allowing them any participation in the choice of procedures. They say they feel "coerced," "dehumanized," or "like robots," or as though the program sponsors do not "respect their individuality." It is true that most teachers seem to derive profound satisfaction from seeing that a teaching technique works— that the children in their care are indeed learning. As Resnick notes:

You can follow the progress of each child in detail. This has turned out to have very salutary effects, not only for the children—we believe it's been our major instrument for keeping teachers turned on. They see the bar graph growing that records the things the kids have learned to do. And boy, do they love it. When we invented a more visual form of record-keeping, our teacher performance went way up.

This satisfaction may be enough to sustain teacher morale for extended periods, and some programs rely upon it almost exclusively. But sooner or later, even in the best and most effective programs, there is some degree of teacher revolt, or at least passive resistance in the form of diminished effort, unless means can be found of involving the teachers at a higher level.

A number of directors have been experimenting with ways and means to give the teachers scope for their individual initiative and knowledge without allowing the program to lose its focus. Weikart, for example, has been attempting to give teachers increased freedom to choose tasks or procedures that they think are best adapted to the individual child or individual parent. For example, during the home visits, when the teacher is working both with the mother and the child, it is up to the teacher to diagnose whether the mother is too domineering or too passive in her usual interactions with the child. With domineering mothers, the teacher will work more directly with the child and attempt to get the mother to observe the child's reactions to certain teaching devices. With passive mothers, the teacher gives more of her attention to trying to get the mother to do the teaching. In the classroom, Weikart is attempting to discover how much autonomy teachers can be given in devising their own methods of teaching a given concept or principle. For example, a teacher can plan during a given week to work on groups of concepts in which one class includes another in a hierarchical fashion (for example, all roses are flowers and all flowers are plants, but the converse is not true). Within this framework she can employ whatever materials she wishes, or make use of situations that arise spontaneously. Some degree of monitoring of the teacher's behavior seems to be needed, however, even for experienced teachers—there are always instances in which the teacher forgets her objective. For example, she may begin talking about dogs with the intention of pointing out that a dog is an animal and that there are other kinds of animals, but she may allow herself to be sidetracked into social-emotional issues (the dog is your friend, he won't hurt you) and will have lost an opportunity to teach the desired concept.

Resnick has found that detailed testing of the children makes it possible to give the teachers a great deal of freedom for innovation:

> We've asked the teachers to invent as they go, and they've gotten a little better at it. The more structure we give the teachers, the

more inventive they become; the more teaching is tied to specific objectives, the more they are able to come up with teaching techniques; and the more ideas we give them with respect to teaching techniques, the easier it is for them to come up with still more. You'll see different things going on in each classroom. We don't have to dictate each step, because we've got the basic structure so closely monitored.

Innovative teaching programs have a voracious appetite for new teaching devices, new materials. Some classroom procedures are "used up" quickly; the children learn all that is to be learned from them and lose interest. Others, such as matrix and lotto game formats, are adaptable to an almost infinite variety of curriculum contents, and their devotees point out that there is a great advantage to using them repeatedly with varied content: Once the child learns the format, it becomes the avenue to successful mastery of a host of problems. Even when a technique could be useful over a long period of time, however, it is frequently true that the teachers use it often and well just after it has been introduced to a classroom, but gradually forget about it and stop using it. Martin Deutsch, who has been developing a program for disadvantaged children in New York, comments:

The monitoring of new procedures is extremely important. Any innovation decays. The more supervision, the longer it lasts. It has been our experience that without close supervision, the halflife of an innovation is about thirteen weeks. With supervision it can maintain itself, so long as there are provisions for allowing the method to change and adapt itself somewhat to the requirements of individual teachers and particular groups of children.

Gordon encourages teachers to invent new teaching tasks; these tasks are then tried out experimentally by the sponsor to see whether they meet the objectives of the project. Some do so only if they are used in a certain way, and procedures for making the optimum use of the task are worked out and transmitted back through the trainers to other teachers. In this way new curriculum materials are constantly being generated by people who have first-hand acquaintance with the kind of task that is most applicable to the particular groups of children being taught.

If teachers are to be effective in innovation, they must have very full understanding of the program's philosophy and the detailed objectives of the curriculum. To achieve this, programs are continuously engaged in teacher training and have experimented with various ways of organizing it. Bushell describes some of the unsuccessful training efforts that have been tried and abandoned in his program:

> We began with a summer institute. We had clear effects on the attitudes of the participants—they loved it. We measured to see whether there was any change in what they were doing in their classrooms after they got home, and found none. So we abandoned summer institutes. The other thing we're taught to do as professionals is to be consultants—wise men who drop in and tell everybody how to do it right. We sent a polished consultant from district to district, and would take data on some specific aspects of teaching and learning before the arrival of the consultant and after his departure. And without knowing [his] travel schedule, we couldn't tell when [he] had been there. So we dropped consultants.

Ultimately, Bushell found that working with individual teachers, giving them detailed feedback about what they were doing, and using demonstration of detailed points was the only answer:

> In one eastern city, the entry point was obtained through sheer desperation. We brought everybody together for three days and literally stood beside each one of them and said, "Do it this way." For some reason it had a huge effect, although there's nothing in my background that suggests that that's an appropriate way to do it.

Bushell recommends working with the teachers individually in their own classrooms for perhaps three days at a time, working on one aspect of teaching technique at a time, and watching for evidence of the desired changes in teacher behavior. The objectives of teacher training must be as carefully specified as the objectives of child teaching. And the emphasis is on providing the teacher with direct encounters, with new ways of organizing the teaching process. Bushell says:

Rather than *talking* about the benefits of parent aides, we can set the occasion for the teacher to *experience* the advantages of this instructional help. In short, we now arrange for the teacher to have some guaranteed success, and we are learning how to take advantage of the fact that almost all teachers are reinforced by the achievements of their children.

Teachers' Aides ✳

As mentioned earlier, all programs agree on the importance of individualizing instruction to the greatest possible degree. It is never possible to provide enough trained, "accredited" teachers per classroom to provide very much one-to-one instruction. Some programs have turned primarily to automated teaching devices, such as the preprogramed typewriter, or nonautomated but high-feedback instructional materials, such as the "Language Master," to increase the amount of "teaching" that goes on when the teacher cannot be with an individual child. Some programs (notably Gotkin's games, EDC, and the Tucson project) have attempted to involve the children in teaching one another through use of teaching materials that make it possible for the children who already know how to handle the materials to help the ones who do not.

Most programs, however, have expanded the teaching personnel by employing teachers' aides. The teachers' aides are not added simply because they increase teaching manpower; they are often parents of children enrolled in the program. In programs where this is not a requirement, the aides are nevertheless chosen from the community and share the racial, ethnic, and social-class characteristics of the families being served by the program. It is hoped that the benefits of improved teaching and improved understanding of how children learn will extend beyond the Follow-Through classroom into the homes of the aides and into the contacts the aides have with other parents and other children not involved directly in the program. Beyond this, in the programs where the aides are genuine participants in curriculum development, it is hoped that the aides can bring special talents to the improvement of teaching through their first-hand knowledge of the culture in which the children have grown up.

The introduction of teachers' aides into the classroom is often attended by strains and difficulties from the standpoint of the regular teacher. As Bushell notes:

> It is not difficult to understand that not all teachers have taken kindly to the idea of having parent aides instructing "their" children. We were told directly by some teachers that they felt uncomfortable and did not trust the parents to teach the children.

A number of people have commented on the difficulty of getting the aides involved in *teaching,* as distinct from simply performing caretaking functions in the classroom. Gordon explicitly watches for this:

> Our program is to convince both the teacher and the principal that the parent educator *can* do teaching. If we see the aides standing around the edge of the classroom, that's a violation of the model. We use Robert Soar's observation schedule for the classroom. We use a list of all the things an adult can do in a classroom—pouring juice, instructing a small group, individual teaching with a child, helping with coats and jackets, etc. Two days a month we observe in a classroom and record who is doing what at various times during the day. We look to see where the activities cluster. If the parent educator is doing nothing but cleaning up the tables, we know something is wrong. Actually, we don't have this trouble too much. The parent educators are doing fine and we are very happy with what they are doing. It's the teachers who are most likely to have morale problems.

In programs where aides have successfully learned to teach according to the program's specifications, there appear to have been some unanticipated side effects in the life style of the individuals involved. Gordon says:

> I think it is quite clear that the group we *really* have changed are the group of women who have been trained to train others. Originally, they come out of the same group of mothers. But after they've become teaching aides, they all come in here about eight-thirty in the morning. They dress differently, they talk differently, and you can see that to some degree we've made them upwardly socially mobile.

Gordon is not convinced that such effects are an unmixed blessing, since they may create a degree of "snobbishness" on the part of the aides toward the people they are supposed to teach—the children and the other mothers.

Coping with School-System Rigidities ✳

Many changes will inevitably occur in the bureaucratic structure of the schools if Follow-Through programs have the impact that they are intended to have. Weikart underlines this point:

> We're not paying enough attention to the aspects of the system which perpetuate the status quo. "Intervention" means that you want to destroy the existing structure. Compensatory education is revolutionary, or should be. We've got to find ways of getting change to stick. A system has got to have self-corrective feedback, or [change] won't be self-maintaining. I think we need people like systems analysts—maybe even military analysts!—to think about the characteristics of school systems that are thwarting our change efforts, and to help us see how the system can be made to respond.

We heard many poignant illustrations of the sluggishness of school systems when faced with demands for change. Things that seem relatively simple—like getting permission to rearrange the furniture in a classroom so as to create "interest areas" for teaching several small groups of children at one time—turn out to be something to which there is resistance. Sometimes it is difficult to locate the source of the resistance, and the program personnel begin to feel they are living in a Kafkaesque world, where unknown conspiracies exist to thwart their programs. The frustration of this situation tempts them to direct action. Indeed, in one school system where the desks are required to be bolted to the floor in every classroom, a program director sneaked in at night with a screwdriver and unbolted the desks, after his plea for a more flexible classroom arrangement had fallen upon deaf ears at every level of the school-system hierarchy. Incidentally, he was given an ovation at the next parents' meeting.

8 *

Community Control

In this chapter we deal with what are essentially political questions—questions about where the power over school systems ought to rest if needed changes are to come about. Many people are now saying that only fundamental changes in the locus of control over schools will overcome the existing inertia of the educational "establishment." The recent confrontation in Ocean Hill–Brownsville, New York, between the school system (both the administrative personnel and the teachers' union) and community representatives is only one of the more visible instances of a drama that is being enacted in most of the urban school systems in the country. The point of view of those who advocate a large measure of decentralization of schools—of community control—is presented by Haskins, a former school principal who was selected by the parents of the school that employed him:

> Right now, I am very much involved in the movement for community control of schools. I am an advocate of it because, like other people in the movement, I came to the conclusion that those who were running the schools had certain problems in dealing with children of minority groups and were unable or unwilling to make those massive changes that seemed necessary in order to change a system enough. When you talk about massive changes, it touches on everything: the textbooks you use, the teachers you hire, how

they're prepared, the way schools are built, and the rules and regulations that are made according to the norms of one community and then foisted upon another community.

The whole movement grew out of many attempts at integration. When it didn't happen, we decided to let black people decide what will happen to them. Up until now, people interested in educating minority-group children have started out by saying, "We want to change teacher attitudes," but they quickly discover that's the hardest thing to change, so they retreat back to making the children acceptable to the teachers. Those involved in community control are refusing to give up on that point. They insist that secretaries in the school have to treat parents with respect, that principals have to treat people with respect, that the schools have to be put on almost a consumer-producer relationship, like most other institutions are, so a parent can say to a school, "Either you service me well, or I get rid of you and go someplace else." The parents are really not saying they know how to be teachers, any more than I know how to be a plumber, but if I ask you to fix a faucet for me and it's still leaking when you leave, I know you didn't do something right and I'll get another plumber next time.

What exactly is meant by "community"? The answer is often unclear. In very large cities control by a minority group may not mean local control by the "consumer parent" in the sense that Haskins describes. When a minority group has won political control of a large segment of a city, a considerable degree of power often becomes centralized in a bureaucratic framework, and parents of a given school may have little influence on the bureaucracy even though the bureaucracy contains many people of the same minority group. This is true in spite of the fact that the major impetus for community control and decentralization comes from the demands of minority groups to control their own affairs.

If a school is to be a community school in the best sense of the word, Haskins believes, it must become a center for many community activities and play a role that goes considerably beyond classroom instruction:

We've attempted to make the school a center which we hope would bring in everybody from the community. We've already set up certain facilities in our school that no others have. What used to be the principal's office is now a clinic that's turned over to Children's Hospital, and it's open every afternoon. It's a community facility. We also put a student unit of social workers into the school. Their role in our school is no longer one of making children adjust to a poor teacher; their job is to help change the social climate in the school so the flow from the community into the school is not a completely alien thing. The definitions of the community are still being made. If I am principal of a school, the parents should be able to have confidence in me that as a black person and as a principal I will be the advocate of their children, even if they're not on my back. But they still have a right to watch me carefully to make sure that I do it.

Haskins stresses the importance of the school's showing *respect* for the child and the minority culture from which he comes. To achieve this, he feels, the school must foster the child's identification with his own group.

Cultural Pluralism ✳

There is a widespread feeling among Follow-Through educators that the schools should not be attempting to transmit only the values and customs of white middle-class America. Manuel Ramirez, who works with Mexican-American children, comments on this point:

My concern has been with the identity conflict and alienation which the school has created in the Mexican-American child, primarily because of schoolpeople's lack of knowledge about the Mexican-American culture. Many of the values which the schools represent are in conflict with those of the Mexican culture, and the schools have valued this culture negatively in the history of the United States. The Mexican-American civil rights movement is fortunately moving in the direction of having more identification with the culture. We don't want to segregate ourselves, but we want our children to be competent in both cultures.

What exactly is meant by saying that teachers should respect the minority-group-child's culture? What difference does it make if the teacher understands it? Alice Paul, a trainer of teachers for Indian schools, illustrates how value differences show themselves in a classroom:

> I've seen teachers take Indian children under the chin, and lift their chin and say, "Look at me when I want to speak to you." Somehow they feel this child is not showing respect because he's looking away. Yet, in the child's own culture, *not* to look at someone is showing respect. And the teacher, not knowing this, is violating the child's upbringing. She's operating in her own culture.
>
> Teachers often like to show affection to children. They put them on their laps, or put their arms around them and that kind of thing, and here again, emotion in many of the Indian tribes is something that is not expressed in public. Even physical contact is something that you don't do. In growing up, I knew that love existed between my mother and father, even though it was not publicly displayed. It was understood, it was accepted. We did not have to be told constantly that we were loved—it was there.

Clearly, the implication of these remarks is that the child could adjust more easily to the school if the teacher understood the values of the child's home and community and behaved in ways that were consistent with them.

It has been widely assumed that one way to ensure respect for the child's culture is to hire teachers who come from the same minority group. It is undoubtedly true that there is usually greater understanding between people who share a similar cultural background. Furthermore, the very presence of such teachers in the schools promotes the children's pride in their own group and is helpful in providing high-status models with whom they can identify. Nevertheless, it sometimes happens that the minority-group person who has managed to educate himself and achieve a good standard of living will reject his own origins and be very intolerant of the children's dialects, manners, and life styles. As Gotkin says:

> I've found teacher resistance to the introduction of black music. Interestingly this happened in different ways in two communities. In

a northern city, the problem was that most of the teachers were white, and they were not familiar with the beat. But in a southern town, it was quite different. The black teachers there, having risen to middle-class status, have rejected much of their own history.

The racial origins of the teacher, then, are not the only factors to be taken into account in an attempt to achieve better communication with the child in relation to his own value system.

In classes of Indian or Mexican-American children, of course, whether the teacher can use or understand the child's native language is of paramount importance. Alice Paul reports that there are teachers who have worked with Indian children for over twenty years and still don't know how to say, "Good morning," or "Why are you crying?" or "Do you have to go to the bathroom?" in the children's language. Ramirez comments:

> In many school districts in the Southwest, Mexican-American children are not allowed to speak Spanish in the schools. In these districts, too, the drop-out rate among Mexican-American students before they reach the twelfth grade is 40 to 50 percent. In some school districts it reaches 70 or 80 percent. Their educational attainment is about three years below that of blacks, and about four to six years below that of the whites. Yet there is very little done to try to build an educational program that is based on the Mexican-American culture, on the style of learning and language that the child brings with him to school.

The drive toward cultural pluralism has profound implications. It stands in direct opposition to the "melting pot" tradition that has been taken for granted in American education for over a century. There are also implications for school integration. Can one teach Mexican-American children in Spanish if only a few children in the classroom come from Spanish-speaking homes? Must one put them in separate classrooms in order to teach them in a way that is consistent with their backgrounds? People who advocate the introduction of "black studies" often claim that it is good for white children as well as black ones to know something about black history and culture. They say that this kind of cultural pluralism is consistent with school integration. Nevertheless, when such programs have been introduced at the high-school and college levels, blacks have sometimes preferred to exclude white students from them. They see these curriculum elements as part of the process of forging racial identity and racial pride, and feel that this process occurs more effectively in segregated groups.

For the most part, the advocates of community control work within a framework of segregated schools. Some educators are deeply alarmed over what they see as a trend toward resegregation. They fear that efforts to achieve community control will lead further in this direction. However, Richard Dunham, working in a southern community, believes that community control can be achieved without sacrificing the goal of integration:

> We operate with half white and half Negro participants. We've gone to some lengths to make sure there is no staff position that's marked by color. We went into a community where many people thought it would not be practical to run a fully integrated whole-family-involvement project, but simultaneously, we have achieved physical integration and autonomy, with the parents, white and Negro, relating to each other in a physically integrated program. There has been acceptance of integration; friendships developed across racial lines, primarily between the children, but secondarily among families as a whole. The families have sponsored integrated parties of their own.

Many black people are profoundly skeptical about there being any significant momentum toward genuine integration in the nation's schools at present. They do not want to wait for integration as the primary avenue for improvement in the education of black children. Haskins says:

> The school that I have, I found segregated when I came. My contention has always been that I will make a school a good school for whatever children are there. I believe that it will be a good school for white children also. We do not use anything that's against white people in order to make black people feel good about themselves. There are certain problems—if a parent calls it a

problem—that a white child finds in the school, and that's because he's in a minority. A parent said to me that I was emphasizing black history. My answer was, "If your child was educated in China, you'd come back bragging that he was educated in China, and he would have learned Chinese history, and you would have taken care to teach him whatever else you wanted to teach him." I did not intend to be abusive to her child, but if her child was in this school, in some ways he would have a broader education if she saw to it herself, rather than to get me to tailor a school that's 99.9 percent black to her one or two white children that are in the school. If there were more white children in the school, it would alter its character accordingly. I don't intend, at this time of my life, to put any more energy into integration, when people run so fast when you try to catch up with them.

Whether the efforts toward community control and participation proceed in a context of segregation or integration, there are stumbling blocks at many points, and often only the appearance, not the reality, of change. Ramirez comments that, even though the Follow-Through Guidelines require that the community shall have a voice in planning, the parents often have little real influence and are consulted only as a matter of form after the decisions have been made:

Mexican-Americans have been left out of the planning of programs for themselves. Recently in a southwestern city, a parent-child center was being established by the university, and after the plans were set up, they brought in people from the community and said, "Here it is, approve it."

In areas of the deep South, black activists are demanding greater control over all kinds of public services to and for black people: police, welfare, public health, and, of course, education. But while in some areas black neighborhoods are now patrolled by black police, the black schools are still controlled by all-white school boards. One project director reports about one of his school districts:

They still have the publicly elected school board, all white, all land-owners, businessmen, and so forth, running an almost totally black school system. Here the white community is very paternalistic. It uses clever ways to maintain control. For example, in the business of finding program assistants for our projects, they can't somehow reach the decision. The day of crisis, when we absolutely have to have the person on the job, is coming very rapidly. Then, by golly, just the day before the appointment has to be made, they'll make an emergency appointment who'll just happen to turn out to be white.

In the Middle: Project Follow-Through ✳

The Follow-Through project director often finds himself in the very center of the interracial power struggle. He often finds that his own activities are part of a revolutionary force, and he cannot avoid taking sides, even if he should want to. It can be enormously diffi-cult to decide how to be an *effective* force for change, however; there is always the danger that his activities will boomerang and jeopardize the very people he would like to help. One project di-rector describes working in one southern setting where the blacks are numerically in the minority and the whites are "red necks" with openly racist attitudes:

It doesn't have the flavor of the White Man's Burden, as in Mis-sissippi, or the subtlety of the sophisticated New Yorker. It's ex-tremely hard on our staff there—you listen, and you don't know what to do. Do you blow the whole program, or do you cast your-self as the insidious secret agent who's going to undermine the system over time? We need to be sensitive to the people who live right there, and only go as far as they go. If the local blacks choose to back down, that's as far as we can go. We take our cues for our relationship with the whites on the race issue by what the blacks tell us to do.

There have been a number of instances in which the growth of community control of school systems has meant increased support for Follow-Through programs. Parents are impressed by results. If a child who has been afraid or bored in school becomes enthusiastic about going to school in the morning, and comes home in the afternoon with excited reports about the things he has been learning, his parents will support the change in the school program that brought this about, if they are in a position to do so. There are instances in which parent groups have insisted on the continuation of Follow-Through programs when school administrations were ready to discontinue them.

However, it would be naive to assume that community power always leads directly to increased support of whatever Follow-Through people want to do. Specifically, there has been a good deal of opposition from community leaders to the research and evaluation aspects of compensatory education programs. Joan Costello, of the Institute of Juvenile Research, reports that in a very impoverished area of Chicago, where most community services were at a low ebb, a research group helped to organize community action groups, including an advisory group to help oversee their own research work. Initially, the "advisory" group tended to rubber-stamp the research group's plans. But after the assassination of Dr. Martin Luther King the mood changed:

> By fall we had the first questions about "What are you doing?" Not, "We don't understand"—there's never been any real question about whether people *understood* what we were doing. When parents were asked to sign a release for a small medical project, one mother said she would not sign it. She said she understood what we were doing, but that there had been a lot of research on black people, and very little had come of it, and it was time to stop being accepting until people could deliver more than a minimal service in return. She brought this up at a parents' meeting, which was awful from the point of view of doing research, but was magnificent from the point of view of community organization.

There is a fairly widespread feeling among certain parent groups that precious time and resources should not be spent in further fact-finding—that we already know enough as a basis for action, and the resources should be directed toward actual services to needy people. Furthermore, there is resentment that compensatory education funds should be contingent on research findings while services to the prosperous parts of the community are not. Haskins comments about this:

> There are people involved in a program like Head Start who have their own children in [private] nursery schools. They have them there because they think it's a good program. They'll take them out if they don't like it, and they never ask Westinghouse to do any research to find out whether the program is working. Even if it only means that their wife can have two hours off in the morning, they consider it enough. But they have put poor people's children into a kind of nursery-school program and have told them that *they* (the program funders) will decide whether it's doing what they think it should do for the poor people's children, and if it's not, they'll stop it. Yet they still have their own children in nursery school. What does that mean for the way they feel about other people's children?

The growth of community power can mean other restraints on Follow-Through programs. Parents are usually (not always) content to leave matters of teaching method to the experts. But when it comes to the question of *what* shall be taught, they will be closely interested. Indeed, as Haskins says, the more effective they think a teaching program is, the more vigilant they will feel they must be:

> Maybe the more successful you are, the more frightening it is. Engelmann tells me he can teach a kid to do whatever he wants him to, and if it's my kid, I have to watch Engelmann very carefully. I'm not sure what he wants to teach my kid, particularly if he's not from the group I come from. All I know is that in eighteen hundred it was against the law to teach black kids to read and write. White people made those laws. And here comes someone who tells me they can make my kid do whatever they want to. And I remember the gas chambers in Germany, and think about the rumors that are going around that Job Corps is being put aside so the sites can be used as concentration camps. Or people will say, "Bereiter-Engelmann *trains* black children, but they want to *educate* white children to teach them how to read and how to think."

It is difficult to say how pervasive these concerns are among leaders of minority groups, but it does seem clear that real shifts in the locus of control over educational institutions will inevitably change the nature of the things that can—or perhaps should—be done in Follow-Through programs. One sponsor says:

> As I see it, I've only got about two more years to make this program work. After that, they're not going to want to see any more white faces around here. If by that time I haven't convinced the local people that this approach is worth doing, and trained them how to do it, I might as well forget it.

Which brings us to the central question of how any innovations that Follow-Through programs bring into being can become part of the normal educational process. These programs are endeavoring to find effective methods of teaching the children of the poor; they are endeavoring to find out how to get school systems to accept these changes. But their ultimate objective is to put themselves out of business. They hope to change schools and teaching practices so fundamentally that the improvements will be self-perpetuating and will maintain themselves after Follow-Through has come to an end.

9 *

Epilogue

We said in the Preface that this report was not an effort to evaluate the accomplishments of Follow-Through, and we noted that the children in these programs (along with comparison groups of children *not* in the programs) are being tested now. Whatever the outcome of these evaluations, it is likely that the press will tend to oversimplify and stereotype the findings. Headline writers will be tempted to catch the eye of the reader with arresting phrases such as: "Project Follow-Through: Overwhelming Success," or "Compensatory Education Has Failed." One can be reasonably certain in advance that no encapsulating statement of this sort can possibly be true.

Success is never an all-or-nothing affair. In the first place, one program is likely to make progress toward certain objectives while having little impact on other objectives that policy-makers may deem important; another program may prove to have quite different strengths and weaknesses. Furthermore, the progress of educational programs occurs step by step. The space program provides an analogy: It proceeded by developing a capsule and a launching rocket, testing them, discovering their defects, correcting them and producing a new version, testing *that,* and so on. In the same way, experimental educational programs need to be continuously re-engineered on the basis of feedback that is obtained from each successive modification of the program.

Research that is geared to the stepwise testing of a program in this way is not always compatible with the kind of research that is needed for policy decisions at the highest level about the fate of an entire program. Periodically, the Congress and the President's office must make decisions about whether funding for the whole cluster of experimental programs will be continued. Their decision is usually of a fairly sweeping sort: whether to support the program at existing levels, expand it, or phase it out. Such decisions are triggered by the President's budget message to Congress and Congressional action on appropriation bills. The timing has little relation to the actual time requirements and growth phases of the work to be done.

There has been a tendency in recent years for rather erratic, large-scale swings in public policy to occur in brief periods of time. A remedial program, such as Head Start, or a vocational training program for the hard-core unemployed, is first presented by its advocates as a powerful cure-all for a wide range of social ills. Indeed, its potential advantages probably *must* be exaggerated if the program is to have a chance of adoption in the first place. But the program has little chance of accomplishing quickly the unrealistic objectives set forth for it, and there follows a period of disillusion; support for the program dwindles away, and new competing programs absorb the available resources before there has been time for the original program to show what it *can* do.

Compensatory education is intrinsically a very difficult process. It involves all the ills of the urban slums and all the tensions of the current interracial situation. Attempts to reform school systems, if they occur without simultaneous change in other social institutions, will surely not be enough to meet the problems of the minority-group child. But they are a place to start.

We are only beginning to understand the reasons why most existing schools are ineffective in educating poor children. We have not yet identified dependable remedies. This is a situation that calls for innovation—for experimentation with a wide range of methods, including some fairly radical departures from the traditional ways of doing things. People who think they know some solutions should have a chance to try them out, if they can convince local communities that their plans are worth trying.

There are some vigorous, innovative, experimental programs going on now. Competing educational philosophies are being put to the test on a scale that is truly unique in the history of American education. We believe these experiments deserve time and room to work in. We are not arguing that they should be immune to scrutiny. Indeed, continual evaluation is essential if the programs are to know precisely where they have succeeded and in what respects they need to change. Furthermore, their work cannot proceed at a leisurely pace. The problems are too urgent for that. The knowledge that a program will have to demonstrate results after a reasonable time undoubtedly provides a needed spur and helps keep up momentum in the face of pressures to relax and let things drift back to the tried and true ways of doing things.

But any program must go through an upheaval when it first faces the realities of life in ghetto schools. The experimental educator must learn to listen to the voice of the community; he must build a stock of teaching materials and add to his repertoire of teaching techniques; he must build staff and accumulate "know-how" in training teachers and working out relationships with existing school-system personnel; he must learn from his early mistakes. It is only after these initial phases have been endured that there is real hope for demonstrable results on a significant scale. It sometimes turns out that there are serious impediments to educational innovation in the form of state rules and regulations, or even state legislation, and these restrictions may be susceptible to change only after the experimental educator has demonstrated at least modest results in the early phases of his program. When they are changed, the possibilities for discovery and increased progress in the later phases are enhanced.

It is tragic if programs are cut off just when they have emerged from these first phases. It is imperative that there be a steady base of support throughout the early days and into the program's maturity. Policy-makers must somehow withstand the pressures from those who want instant results. Americans are accustomed to making investments in "research and development" in private industry and in public enterprises such as the military departments of our government. Surely the public will be prepared to support a continuing program of experimental research and development in education as well, if the case is clearly put. There is growing public concern over our "national priorities." Here is a good place to redress the balance.

INDEX ✳

A 0
B 1
C 2
D 3
E 4
F 5
G 6
H 7
I 8
J 9